Anatomy of the Wine Trade

Anatomy of the Wine Trade

Abe's Sardines and Other Stories

SIMON LOFTUS

Edited and introduced by Jancis Robinson

1817

HARPER & ROW, PUBLISHERS, New York
Cambridge, Philadelphia, San Francisco, Washington,
London, Mexico City, São Paulo, Singapore, Sydney

FIRST U.S. EDITION

Library of Congress Cataloging-in-Publication Data

Loftus, Simon.
   Anatomy of the wine trade.

   Includes index.
   1. Wine industry.   I. Robinson, Jancis.   II. Title.
HD9370.5.L64   1987   380.1′456632   87-45066
ISBN 0-06-015785-2

87 88 89 90 91 HC 10 9 8 7 6 5 4 3 2 1

For my father

Contents

Acknowledgements

Unless a large number of my friends had agreed to let me write about them (reckless insanity some might think), this book would not have been possible. To all of them, many thanks.

I am also grateful to the Editor of *Vogue* for permission to reprint parts of an article that I wrote for the 'Wine Days' feature, and to the Editor of the trade magazine, *Wine & Spirit*, for agreeing to let me use some material that originally appeared there and to quote an extract from 'Foubert's Diary'.

Susannah Collings, my secretary at Adnams, typed and retyped from my handwritten manuscript, patiently accepting numerous afterthoughts and corrections. She also made plenty of comments as it went along, many of which I took gratefully to heart. She was indispensable.

Preface

'He was living proof that every family tree must have its sap.'

Buster Keaton: *The Navigator*

The arms trade is profitable but has the seedy glamour that adheres to fashionable criminals. Banking is respectable but dull. Two world wars and the nuclear threat have taken the glossy dash off a military career, and the life of a spy is probably unique in combining the disadvantages of danger and tedium. The clergy may be telling the truth but are rarely believed, while journalists and lawyers tell lies which sound entirely credible.

The choice of profession is full of problems. No wonder that doting parents and their indolent offspring find themselves dreaming, so often, of the wine trade. It has, after all, a long tradition of providing an occupation, if not a living, for amiable nincompoops. What could be more agreeable, it would seem, than travelling abroad to visit famous châteaux and returning home with wonderful wines, which you taste in the morning with a few well-heeled customers before adjourning for a leisurely lunch, accompanied by a series of venerable bottles? The reality is otherwise.

In the first place, the tasting of young wine is often a thoroughly disagreeable occupation requiring both skill and stamina. Standing in a dank cellar at nine o'clock on a cold February morning, trying to make some sense of the raw astringency of a dozen cask-samples of four-month-old claret, it is possible to doubt one's vocation. At the end of the day, having spat out forty or fifty young wines, and written notes on their future development which owe more to clairvoyance than sensory analysis, such doubts congeal into a sense of overwhelming weariness. The idea of a bowl of soup, a hot bath and bed seems infinitely more appealing than the reality of dinner at the latest expensive restaurant with the chain-smoking export director of a multi-national group.

To such moments of tedium are added the problems of floating exchange rates, and the difficulties of a commodity market which depends on the vagaries of climate and agricultural good fortune. You can find yourself floundering in a quicksand of uncertainties. But just as fashion can elevate the rag trade to *haute couture*, so these variables of weather and economic circumstance provide the necessary air of capricious mystique, endowing experts in wine with the glamour of fortune-tellers.

Such glamour (and the intrinsic attractions of the product itself) should not be allowed to disguise the fact that the wine trade is no way to make money. Dedicated imbibers (like followers of fashion) are almost bound to have extensive overdrafts, and are liable to follow the old tradition of placing bills from tailor and wine merchant at the bottom of the pile. The wine trade does not pay very well.

There are splendid, romantic tales of great financial coups, of clever deals or ingenious swindles that have made millions for those involved. Such things happen, of course, but the truth is generally closer to the dictum enunciated by Bernie Turgeon, a wine producer in California, whose money was made in construction and real estate. 'If you want to be a millionaire in the wine business, you first have to be a multi-millionaire in some other trade.'

Wine, nonetheless, is great fun. It is more varied and more interesting than most commodities, and its study involves an appreciation of many things to do with geography, history and culture. Above all, it is inseparable from traditions of hospitality and the enjoyment of good company. For these reasons, perhaps, it attracts the most fascinating range of characters. The wine trade accommodates ruddy-faced peasant growers as comfortably as pale professional gamblers, dedicated enthusiasts and amiable rogues. Some are insufferable scoundrels, but a good many of them have come to be my treasured friends. For better or worse they have inspired this book.

It will be immediately apparent that the result is a long way from being a clinical dissection of the wine trade, laying bare its component parts and demonstrating their inter-relationships. Instead, it is a collection of portraits of individuals; a series of short stories, the settings for which are various stages on the often tortuous journey between vine and glass.

At first sight this may seem too fragmentary an approach, but the observant reader will soon notice a surprising number of connections, linking these disparate parts. He will come to realize that the wine trade, despite its international ramifications, is rather small and quite densely tied together.

This is, of course, a highly personal book – a documentary of my own working life in the trade, running the wine division of Adnams Brewery. For these are my suppliers, my agents, my rivals and customers. It is a true picture, but incomplete, both for reasons of space and time, and because I decided at the outset to concentrate on what I value – quality and individuality – and to ignore the shoddy and depressing anonymity of large areas of the mass market.

The wine trade, in any case, deserves affectionate treatment, for it is still imbued with traditions of great generosity. Fierce competitors regularly send each other samples, exchange information and share treasured bottles together, wines that were bought years ago and are now worth a fortune. The fact that the merchants prefer to enjoy with their friends what they could otherwise sell at great profit is thought extremely foolish by the accountants. But these are very amiable fools.

Simon Loftus

Foreword

Simon Loftus is probably the only wine merchant in the world who is an accomplished stilt-walker. (Why, with his height he should bother, I cannot imagine, but that is another matter.) Much more important, however, he is the only wine merchant I have ever met who is a natural writer. His wine lists are models of enthusiastic anecdote and opinionated counsel, the lot presented in irresistible prose. (I believe I was once tempted sufficiently to read his conditions of sale.)

In this book he demonstrates that the wine trade is so much more than the simple business of making and selling a product. For the first time ever, he puts a wickedly human face on the unique *cuvée* of peasant vine-growers, haughty château-owners, wily wine-brokers, purveyors of wine to the gentry, canny supermarket buyers, smooth auctioneers, and even prickly wine writers that constitutes the wine trade. Major career changes are envisaged, both into and out of the trade in question, for those who read this book.

Anatomy of the Wine Trade will provide pleasure and insight even to a reader with no knowledge of wine at all, while those with a passing or deeper acquaintance with the world's winescape (and there are characters here from all over the wine world) should be riveted by this perceptive and highly idiosyncratic portrait of an enviable way of earning a living.

Jancis Robinson

I

The Beginning and the End of the Wine Trade

Tradition and Change

The wine trade is founded on ancient traditions. The world of many small growers is recognizably that which the Roman poet Virgil described two thousand years ago, and his advice on viticulture still has the force of practical experience. But the small-scale husbandry of the *Georgics* is rapidly being superseded by organizations of a quite different sort. While Virgil would have felt at home on the Piedmontese farm of Guido and Virginia Stra, he would certainly have been mightily amazed by the technological complexity of Villa Banfi, the most dynamic wine group in Europe.

A company of this sort is a new phenomenon, a product of the turmoil of the last twenty years that has tended to break down the highly stratified structure of the traditional trade. It is worth summarizing these changes before looking in detail at the almost archaic life of the Stras, and the headlong progress of Villa Banfi, and all that lies between.

Wine is an agricultural crop. Novices are bemused by the apparent complexities of vintage and vineyard, vine variety and yield. The whole picture becomes much clearer if you think of potatoes.

Potatoes share with the vine a general preference for well-drained land, which is not over-rich in nutrients. For reasons of soil or microclimate, they do better in some fields than in others.

Choice of variety is important. There are heavy-cropping potatoes which can be sold cheaply but which don't taste as good as the lower-yielding, but more expensive, varieties with exotic names, like Pink Fir Apple. The big-croppers tend to be hardy, resistant to disease, while the others are more difficult to grow and susceptible to every sort of problem. You can make plonk on a vast scale from the Carignan grape, but it is much harder to find a vineyard in which the Pinot Noir grape will really thrive.

There is a commodity market in potatoes, just as there is in wine, because the harvest of each is dependent on the weather. A great vintage is, simply, a year in which the grapes have formed healthy bunches on the vine after a successful flowering in the spring, and have received sufficient rain and sunshine to enable them to ripen by the time they are picked in the autumn. Just as potatoes can fail to develop properly if it is too cold and wet (or too dry), and are subject to a variety of pests and diseases, so too with the vine. These are the sort of considerations that fill the minds of all farmers, wine-growers included.

In addition to these general problems, however, the wine-grower must consider the implications of a good many agricultural techniques that have revolutionized the practices of his ancestors. There are still some smallholders who regard their art as a mystery, who follow without question the methods of their forefathers, organizing their work in conjunction with the phases of the moon. Such beliefs (however soundly based) are increasingly rare.

The modern grower may well attend a seminar at which the topics include clonal selection and tissue culture; optimum spacing between rows; the best methods of pruning; T-budding versus chip-budding; the side-effects of anti-rot sprays. All these matters involve questions of quality, which have to be balanced against the economic benefits of greater yield, and the increased mechanization of cultivation and harvesting.

For many growers this is enough to cope with. They sell their grapes to a co-operative or *négociant*, and have nothing to do with the business of actually making wine. Others, however, wish to exercise control over what they produce, from vineyard to bottle.

Vinification, like cooking, was discovered by accident. The brother of the hunter who brushed the ashes off a leg of deer that he had dropped in the fire was the man who forgot about a jar full of grapes at the back of his cave. The grapes were broken, their juice fermented and a few cautious sips led to the first hangover. Several thousand years of experimentation and improvement transformed burnt leg of deer into roast haunch of venison, and the fermented juice of wild grapes into fine wine.

The practice of wine-making is thus very ancient, but it was not until Louis Pasteur in the nineteenth century that some of its most essential principles were understood. Since then, there has been a continuing process of experimentation in both laboratory and winery, aimed at replacing the intuitive traditional methods by modern systems of technological control. What has been regarded as the art of wine-making is being taken over by the scientist.

At its best this leads to the 'anything's possible' attitude that has enabled a lot of good wine to be produced in unpromising circumstances. In particular, expensive but effective cooling systems have vastly improved the quality of white wine production in warm climates. Sometimes, however, the exponents of the new methods make scornful play with the traditional 'superstitions'. It is certainly true that the traditionalists may give all sorts of cock-eyed explanations for what they do but they still manage to produce great wine. However specious the arguments used to justify them, the classic methods are based on the empiricism of history, whereby that which doesn't work is discarded.

Much of this apparent conflict merely expresses the age-old prejudices of fathers, who believe that the world is going to the dogs, and sons who mutter impatiently about 'old fogeys'. In practice, most of the great wine-makers combine elements of both approaches, even in an area of such grand traditions as Burgundy. They will open the doors of a medieval barn to reveal gleaming devices of stainless steel.

If the work of inquisitive scientists has led to a greater understanding of the process of making wine, it has also enabled the grower to respond to the evolving demands of the consumer, for the worldwide explosion of wine consumption has been accompanied by changes in taste; an increasing preference for lighter, fresher wines in general, and for white wine in particular. Fewer and fewer people are prepared to endanger their livers with the heavy, alcoholic rotgut that used to be the staple produce of southern Europe, and which now has to be distilled if the wine lakes of the Common Market are not to overflow. Quality continues to improve because bad wine is unsaleable at any price.

There is a clamour for 'authenticity', which has found expression in the desire for some sort of legal guarantee (often worthless), and a preference for wines bottled at source, by the producer. Greatly improved methods of transportation mean that it is now possible to satisfy such predilections: it is frequently less expensive to ship wine in bottle than to transport it in bulk. As a result, the expertise of the merchant in maturing, blending and bottling wine has, to a large extent, become redundant.

In the distribution of wine, supermarkets have come to play an important role, coinciding with the world-wide repeal of laws which enabled wholesalers and retailers to impose high prices on the consumer. In response to such competitive pressures, a new breed of adventurous importer has developed. They are expert tasters, fluent in at least one foreign language, who travel widely in the wine-producing countries, attempting to deal direct with the producers, rather than pay the margins that supported the numerous links in the traditional chain of distribution. If middlemen have survived at all, they have had to work harder and for lower percentages.

These changes will be illustrated in future chapters, but to begin with I should like to talk about the ancient world of wine-making that still survives, little altered, to this day. We may be the last generation to know this world directly, to witness the localized, domestic operations that have characterized most wine production for the past two thousand years.

A great deal of this production is untouched by the wine trade, and is the activity of peasant farmers who make wine for themselves and their friends, and perhaps sell a little to others in the immediate locality. At vintage time in Italy, for example, you will find tiny, old-fashioned basket presses standing outside minute *cantinas* (wine cellars) in the back streets of most country villages. The aroma of the fermenting juice mixes satisfactorily with the rich animal odours of the farmyard. The grapes may well have been transported from vineyard to cellar in wicker baskets piled on wooden carts, drawn by white oxen. These are images reminiscent of medieval tapestries.

Such production is often quite outside the controls and record-keeping that form part of the cumbersome apparatus of legality. The wine is made to be drunk within a year of the vintage, two years at most. It may have a regional name but essentially it is just wine, *'vino'*; as necessary and as simple as bread.

In a wine region of some renown there will be a little more care taken, a little more pride in the end result, but the essentials are much the same. Wine is back where it started, as one of the most basic and most widespread of agricultural crops.

Guido and Virginia Stra

'Hard work is the only remedy, so give your praise to a large estate; be content to farm a small one.'

Virgil: *Georgics II*

Guido and Virginia Stra own a few hectares of land near the village of Novello d'Alba in Piedmont, north-west Italy. Their house is one of a group of small buildings which once formed a tiny hamlet but is now uninhabited except for the Stras themselves and various relatives, living in Turin, who have converted the simple homes of their ancestors into weekend cottages. At one end of the Stras' house is a vast pile of logs (fuel for the kitchen stove) and a cluster of rabbit-hutches. The rabbits are bred for eating. Here, opposite the chicken-run, is the sheltered corner where Nono Luigi, Guido's father, used to sit chopping the kindling, and smoking the cigarettes that were forbidden indoors. Veteran of numerous, long-forgotten campaigns and an expert hunter for white truffles (the gastronomic speciality of this region), Nono Luigi died recently at the age of ninety-two.

At the other end of the house is the wine cellar, and nearby is the cattle shed, home of two or three white cows and their calves. The cattle are never permitted to trample on their grazing. Each evening, Guido goes out with a scythe to cut the verges of lanes and meadows. The sweet-smelling mixture of grass and dandelions is piled onto a large cloth with a wooden rake, and bundled up ready to be carried home to the cattle.

In various corners of the house are sacks of grain and hazelnuts; in others stand jars of preserved peaches and cherries and bright red peppers. Lemons grow on trees in tubs in front of the building, and the kitchen garden is full of every kind of vegetable. There are a few rows of flowers and innumerable pots of geraniums.

The setting sounds idyllic and, indeed, it is; but for Guido and

Virginia it also represents great and continuous hard work. The farm is very small, barely sufficient to provide a living. Were it not for the fact that some of their vines produce the treasured Barolo – a wine that commands a good price – theirs would be a life entirely without luxuries, hovering on the borderline of subsistence. As it is, Guido and Virginia rise very early and work together in the fields from dawn to dusk. They have no sons to help them and, unless either of their daughters marries a local boy who is willing to continue the traditional ways, this will be the last generation for their farm, as for many others.

Their house will become a holiday home and their land will be absorbed into a larger agricultural unit. Monoculture of maize or vine will replace the present rich diversity of crops. The lovely fields of dandelions and the extraordinary variety of wild flowers will vanish. The patterns of work, of cultivation, of landholding which have formed the character of this land over the centuries are already changing and will soon disappear.

Today, however, is not a moment for such forebodings. It is a bright day in October and the vintage is in full swing. On all the hillsides in the neighbourhood, the farmers and their families and friends are out gathering the harvest, and the roads are busy with carts carrying grapes to the *cantinas*. Guido and Virginia have already harvested their Dolcetto grape, the 'little sweet' that makes the delicious everyday wine of this region. Today we are to help them pick the last rows of Barbera, a variety that makes a lean, astringent wine, much prized locally.

Guido has a little all-purpose vehicle, a mechanical chameleon. The front is detachable and can be bolted onto a variety of ploughs and other implements, or used as the power-source for a small crusher/stemmer in the cellar. Today it takes the form of a tractor/trailer and it is up in the vineyards, laden with plastic boxes to hold the grapes. My wife, Irène, and I each grab a box, an apron and a pair of secateurs and bend to our task.

The grapes are ripe and healthy, so we rarely have to cut out rotten or unripe berries. The vines are trained on a combination of poles and wires, not too low, and at first the work seems easy. Gradually, though, our hands and aprons become stained and sticky with juice, our backs start aching, and it becomes increasingly difficult to straighten up at the end of each row. Conversation slackens. The trailer, fully laden, is driven back to the farm by Guido, while Virginia and I continue to snip away at the bunches. The afternoon draws on and the work becomes monotonous. It seems unending but suddenly we realize that we are on the last row, and that it is finished. *'Stanca,'* says Virginia with a grin as the final container of grapes is loaded onto the trailer. *'Stanca!'*: 'Exhausted!'

But we are pleased with ourselves and, back at the farm, Guido and I taste the still-fermenting Dolcetto, picked a fortnight earlier. Bright purple in colour, lively and prickly on the tongue, it is mouth-filling and already delicious – a good omen for the Barbera that we have just harvested.

Guido will not export his wine. He explains that the paperwork is tedious, and that he can easily sell his small production locally, to friends and to the few tourists who find their way to his farm. He and Virginia bottle some of it, when they can spare the time from other tasks, and they keep the rest in big casks until it is needed.

The quality of the wine owes more to skill in viticulture than expertise in vinification. Guido's Barolo is seldom, in my view, representative of the splendid, rich generosity that should characterize this magnificent wine, and his Barbera is sometimes hard and mean. Both suffer from oxidation during their time in cask. The grand wine, the Barolo, is reserved for sipping with visitors after the meal, like a liqueur. It is usually accompanied by sweet cakes or macaroons, a bizarre but surprisingly effective combination, and, in such circumstances, its old-fashioned, somewhat oxidized character seems appropriate.

Guido's Dolcetto, however, can be wonderful – probably because it is a wine that is drunk within a year or two of the vintage and is less exposed to the accidents of a rather haphazard maturation. At its best it combines the lively flavour of fresh grapes with an almond-like bitterness at the finish. I love it, and I suspect that Guido loves it best as well, despite the fact that it is treated as everyday wine to accompany the wonderful pasta that Virginia and her daughter, Laura, make entirely by hand, on a table in the back kitchen.

The Dolcetto reflects for me the frankness and generosity, the simplicity, strength and happiness of Guido and Virginia, two of the finest people I know. It has the same evocative character as certain scents which instantly recall a particular place and particular people. The Dolcetto is localized not just to a region but to one small farm at Loschetti, to one family.

This is wine at the smallest scale of production. It bears as much relation to the wine trade as a few jars of home-made marmalade, bought at a village fête, bear to the grocery business.

Villa Banfi

'All vestiges of earlier buildings were erased and the countryside was subjected to the most rigorous discipline in the process of which hills were moved and levelled, valleys filled or made, and streams detoured and channelled into new waterways. The expenditures appeared to have reached such alarming proportions that even Fouquet became concerned.'

F. Hamilton Hazlehurst: *Gardens of Illusion:*
The Genius of André
Le Nostre

When Fouquet built himself a palace at Vaux-le-Vicomte and employed Le Nostre to design a suitably extravagant setting, he was finance minister to Louis XIV, a position that enabled him to divert enormous sums from his master's treasury to his own grandiose schemes. Even by the corrupt standards of the seventeenth century, peculation on this scale could hardly be overlooked, especially when Fouquet was foolish enough to entertain his monarch at a party of colossal extravagance to mark the completion of a scheme that had employed over eighteen thousand men on its construction. After the last firework had flickered downwards to meet its reflection in the watergardens, the Sun King returned in silence to his own much more modest quarters at Fontainebleau. Within three weeks Fouquet was in gaol, and his estates confiscated by the Crown.

Such a fate is unlikely to befall the Mariani brothers, but their dreams are hardly less grandiose. At Montalcino, in southern Tuscany, they continue to pour millions of dollars into a scheme that has already reshaped the landscape and involved the construction of great buildings. Their aims may be utilitarian (the pleasure-garden is an enormous vineyard, the palace a huge winery) but the enterprise undoubtedly shares with Fouquet's beautiful but ill-judged monument a number of common features.

In both cases there was a masterplan, uniting buildings and landscape, which was imposed from without, as a unity, rather than having evolved by organic growth. Natural features of the terrain were reshaped to conform to an ideal of aesthetic or agrarian perfection. Neither scheme would have been possible without an appropriate alignment of political forces, and each depended on the co-ordinating talents of a man with an unusual capacity for the organization of a great diversity of professional skills: André Le Nostre in eighteenth-century France, and Ezio Rivella in modern Italy. But what really seizes the imagination is the gamble, the sense of flamboyant daring, always close to peril. For in each case the scheme is so big that it establishes its own momentum to grow larger still, multiplying the opportunities for success or failure. It is probable that what, today, seems the inevitable destiny of Fouquet was for him a most unpleasant surprise, for the outcome of all big gambles remains uncertain until the point at which it is finally determined. It is this uncertainty that gives Villa Banfi its glamour and interest. For we really have no means of knowing whether it will be the prototype of the future wine trade or the latest monument to *folie des grandeurs*.

The story has a larger-than-life quality about it, even by the standards of an Italian/American joint production. Two brothers, John and Harry Mariani, own a modest wine distribution business in New York State. Italian in origin, they have a relaxed attitude to wine as a beverage; being American they understand the needs of the market. They decide that what millions of Americans want to drink is something bubbly, slightly sweet, not too alcoholic. At this stage they are thinking of a white wine, but their consultant oenologist in Italy, Ezio Rivella, suggests the *amabile* (sweet) version of Lambrusco, a red sparkler from Emilia-Romagna. A source of supply is found (a big group of Communist-controlled co-operatives), and within a few years Riunite Lambrusco is the biggest selling wine in the world, accounting for 60 per cent of all Italian wine exports to the States, nearly 40 per cent of the total volume of wine imported into America from any source. The House of Banfi (the Mariani brothers, good Italian sons, called the company after their mother) achieves an annual turnover of $250 million.

But the brothers are well aware that every brand has its day, and that red wine sales in the States are static while white wine consumption is surging ahead. Perhaps they are getting tired of gibes about the red wine from a Communist co-operative that is capitalist

America's favourite tipple; in any case they have profits to invest. They revive their original concept, and decide that this time not only will the wine be white, but they will control its production as well as its distribution.

Hence Villa Banfi. They buy vineyards and wineries at Strevi, Acqui and Novi Ligure, in the classic regions of north-west Italy, where they produce Asti Spumante, various Champagne look-alikes, Gavi, Dolcetto and a strange, sweet red sparkler called Brachetto d'Acqui. These are peripheral, however, to the search for a suitable location to produce the white cousin to Lambrusco of which they dream. After two years' research, their consultant, Rivella (now head of Villa Banfi in Italy), decides on the place: Montalcino in southern Tuscany. Guided by him, Harry and John invest over a hundred million dollars in a development that continues to eat up capital but which they have visited, briefly, only twice in the first five years since its inception in 1979.

The choice of Montalcino is very shrewd. The area was already famous for the red Brunello di Montalcino (one of Italy's most expensive wines), but land was cheap and there was plenty of room for new planting. Even better, there were the half-forgotten remnants of a local tradition of cultivating the Moscadello grape, a clonal variant of the Moscato that had already been designated by Rivella as the ideal basis for the type of semi-sweet, fresh but aromatic wine that he wanted to produce. Determined that the new wine should be granted DOC status (the legal 'guarantee' of controlled origin), Rivella had the two-fold advantage of being able to present his case to the legislators as the revival of an ancient tradition, without being encumbered in any way by a detailed set of archaic practices.

The first stage of the plan has worked. From the 1984 vintage, Moscadello di Montalcino is legally recognized as a traditional quality wine, with new rules for its production written by Rivella and rubber-stamped by the authorities.

'We were hoping to use the other helicopter but it's in pieces at the moment.' The PR girl speaks three or four languages without trace of accent and has all the awesome statistics by heart. This is a big, professional organization.

The helicopters are used for spraying the vines, for transporting Rivella to the outposts of his empire and for showing visitors around the estate. The pilot drifts with practised ease across the landscape. We hover above the vast, still incomplete winery and bottling plant, an enormous complex that looks from the air like any other big-scale modern factory. Then we head north, across terrain which was formerly covered with forests of scrub-oak, interspersed with pasture and patches of cereals, olive trees and vines.

All these things have gone. I ask what happened to the olive trees (a protected species in Tuscany), and am told brusquely that they have been replanted elsewhere, that they can survive on land unfit for vines.

We look down now at hills that have been completely reshaped by giant bulldozers. Peaks and hollows have been smoothed away; bare patches of rock have been covered with soil. Irregularities have disappeared and the regraded slopes have a featureless monotony. The bulldozers have been followed by tractors, ploughing a quarter of a million dollars' worth of organic manure into this infertile land. Two reservoirs have been constructed and a third is being scooped-out by huge machines as we fly past. They feed an underground network of irrigation pipes to provide a once-yearly watering in July. And vines have been planted, all identically spaced and trained on Rivella's favourite Casarsa system, a method that allows for maximum mechanization of cultivation and, it was hoped, mechanized harvesting.

At this point they acknowledge a break-down in the masterplan, for the Moscadello grape has proved particularly resistant to mechanical pickers. The bunches are tight and too many grapes remain on the vine after the machine has passed. This unforeseen problem forces Villa Banfi to call upon a team of labourers at vintage time, increasing rather dramatically the costs of gathering the crop.

We cross the northern boundary of the estate and immediately the landscape changes. The unvarying grid of the Banfi vineyards is replaced by the pleasing irregularities of a more primitive agronomy. On the crest of the hill ahead of us is the fortified medieval town of Montalcino and, as we hover over its tiled roofs and narrow, twisting streets, peering down into the vegetable patches that are sheltered by the castle wall, I am forcefully reminded of the contrast between the organic growth that shaped the traditional patterns of this land, and the unlocalized strategies of multi-national business that impose a quite different geometry.

These days you can buy history. Rivella's eye has long been cast on the estate of Poggio alle Mura, not simply for its 1,200 hectares of land (surrounded on three sides by the Banfi vineyards) but for its hilltop castle, a medieval fortress that he wants to turn into a visitors' centre, combining hotel, restaurant, wine museum, tasting-rooms, shops and a sports complex. The owners held out for a long time, but eventually the almost limitless resources at Rivella's disposal proved sufficient to win the day. Two months before my visit the deal had been completed. The bulldozers are now at work on the land and Poggio alle Mura has been renamed Castello Banfi.

Villa Banfi is well on its way to becoming the largest wine estate in Europe. At Montalcino alone they have nearly 3,000 hectares of land, of which a thousand have initially been designated as vineyards (an area greater in size than Nuits-St-Georges, Vosne-Romanée and Gevrey-Chambertin combined). There will always be some wild bits of forest but they also have olive trees, fruit trees and (a highly speculative project) an experimental area where they are attempting to grow the white truffle, so typical of Rivella's homeland, Piedmont. They have built houses for the estate workers, a hangar for the helicopters, three tractor sheds for the vast array of vineyard equipment. And, of course, they have constructed the winery itself.

I could describe the huge facilities at Montalcino – the enormous scale; the gleaming, automated efficiency; the technological marvels of it all. But remarkable though it is, this is not what sets the operation apart. The Gallo brothers in California have a bigger winery (complete with its own bottle factory), and Robert Mondavi, also in California, is probably more advanced in terms of technology. The unique aspect of Villa Banfi is the fact it was built from scratch as part of a unified scheme to produce what the consumers of one particular market were thought to require. Of course, this has been tried before with other products, but rarely with wine; never on this scale; never with the complete vertical integration of Banfi's operation, all the way through from vineyard to final distribution overseas. As an example of how this affects the smallest details, the labels for the new wines have not been designed by Italians (with their highly developed sense of European chic), but by a California agency, specifically for the American market. The whole operation is consumer- rather than producer-orientated, almost the exact reverse of most European wine-making. It treats wine as a beverage, not as art.

Of course there is much talk of quality. Rivella's instructions from the Mariani brothers, way back in 1977, are said to have been quite simple. 'We want the best wines in the world and they should be Italian.' But, clearly, an idea of quality based on what will sell in vast quantities to Americans (ultimate targets are expressed in millions of cases) is some way removed from the perfectionism of the grower who owns a few rows of vines in Puligny-Montrachet.

The real test has yet to come. As I write, most of the new wines have only been produced in small quantity, for trial in Italy, but initial tastings suggest that they appear to conform to the blueprint. The Chardonnay is a big, blowsy wine, with a marked character of new oak, in the California manner. The Pinot Grigio, by contrast, is fresh and light, with a decent level of acidity. The Brunello promises to be good, while the Cabernet has yet to achieve real character (the vines are still very young). And the Moscadello, the real point of the whole operation, is just what the Mariani brothers wanted: light in colour and alcohol; fresh but flowery on the nose; fizzy; fairly sweet. It is not a wine to be treated seriously, and the only barrier to its overwhelming success may prove to be its price, for it is expected to be significantly more expensive than Lambrusco. This might just take it out of the 'pop-wine' market that it seeks to dominate.

Whether Villa Banfi succeeds is as yet uncertain but, whatever the outcome, it is likely to set the pattern for much of the wine trade in the future. The integration of production and marketing; the elimination of middlemen; the readiness to respond to consumer preference: all of these are features that will be inseparable from other attempts to create big-selling brands. But there will always be those who treasure individuality and are resistant to slick marketing; those who regard diversity of choice as a challenge rather than cause for alarm. It may well be that they first discover the pleasure of wine through Banfi's Moscadello or its equivalent, but such simple beverages will soon pall. It is for these people (who learn from experience) that the rest of the wine trade exists.

II
The Smallholders of Burgundy

Traditions Redefined

Burgundy, lying south of Dijon, is the land of the small domaine; a place where vineyards are fragmented by inheritance into tiny holdings, parcelled out row by row amongst innumerable local growers whose horizon extends to the next village, but whose wines command an international reputation.

It is a much more personal place than Bordeaux, that region of grand estates farmed by absentee landlords. In Bordeaux it is rare for the importer, let alone a private buyer, to deal direct with the producer. Most châteaux continue to sell their wine through brokers to the *négociants*, the grand merchants who were traditionally clustered around the Quai des Chartrons. The best growers in Burgundy, however, prefer to know their customers. They only deal with the *négociants* (some of whom are also renowned vineyard-owners) when they wish to dispose of a few casks that fall below their self-imposed standards of quality. 'I sold it to the *négoces*' means that it wasn't good enough to be bottled under the domaine label. They sell direct, these proud smallholders, to foreign merchants, to the great restaurants of France and to private buyers. If they display all the characteristics of intense regional chauvinism, they also have a shrewd sense of the international value of their wine.

Some of these highly individual characters can talk on equal terms with the most innovative and most able of the world's wine-makers, while others are semi-literate peasants whose inherited traditions have been debased by time, and are now no more than a half-understood collection of ancient prejudices. And, inevitably, there are those who regard the reputation of Burgundy as an opportunity for profit rather than a standard to be upheld.

On the whole, things are better than they were. In the old days, before Britain joined the Common Market, the English merchants used to ship Burgundy at half-price without the certificate of origin. At least, they were told it was Burgundy (the 'surplus production'), but frequently it was 'stretched' with wine from other regions, to cut costs and produce a blend that appealed to the merchants' idea of their customers' taste. English consumers got used to a style of Burgundy that bore little relation to the elegance of the real thing ('a good, full-bodied wine' they called it), and they also got used to unrealistically low prices. The shock of readjustment is still being felt, with few merchants able to sell quality Burgundy at the necessarily high price which it commands.

In the States, things were different. The US market always bought with the appellation certificate. From the 1930s onwards, men like Frank Schoonmaker, Robert Haas and Frederick Wildman, substantial pillars of export Burgundy, used to go out to taste and buy wine, paying for it before shipment and generally supporting the growers who were much poorer than they are today. The Americans were prepared to buy what the country produced, unlike the English who tried to mould wines into what their customers wanted.

Nowadays, the legal niceties are more generally observed, but even so there is vast variation in quality. The regional names, the appellations of Burgundy, appear on everything, from the meanest commercial blend to some of the most wonderful bottles that you could ever hope to find. You cannot rely on vineyard or village name; you must know the producers.

Jean Thévenet

Grape-picking is a messy business; hands and clothes get covered with juice. It is thus that Marie-Thérèse, Jean Thévenet's wife, remembers the character of each vintage. 'You can tell it's a good year,' she said in 1982. 'The telephone is sticky, and the blue jeans stand up by themselves.'

The telephone was even stickier in 1983 because the wonderful autumn had hastened the grapes to an exceptional degree of maturity, with high levels of natural sugar. Jean's only concern was that the wine might end up rather high in alcohol. In the week before the harvest, however, the warm, humid weather brought a sudden explosion of *botrytis cinerea*, the 'noble rot'. *Botrytis* shrivels the grapes, concentrating the richness of the juice and converting some of the natural sugars into glycerol. It is welcome in the Sauternes region of Bordeaux, since it is essential to the production of the finest sweet wines, but in Burgundy it is rarely seen, and is generally considered an embarrassment when it appears. Thévenet's neighbours, in the tiny hamlet of Quintaine-Clessé, hurried to harvest their vines before the *botrytis* spread, and resigned themselves to making clumsy, atypical wines, sometimes with noticeable residual sweetness at the finish. They didn't like the look of the apparently 'rotten' grapes, and they left them for the birds.

Jean, however, is a thoughtful man and so he decided to make a *cuvée spéciale*. He sent his pickers out on 30 September, the second day of the harvest, to gather *only* those bunches that were noticeably affected by *botrytis*. The pickers didn't understand what was going on any more than Jean's father who announced that his son was mad. The inspector of the INAO (the organization that enforces the laws of *appellation contrôlée*) went away scratching his head, unable to find anything in the rules that said Mâcon-Villages had to be dry. The law-makers, presumably, had never considered that anyone would make it sweet.

Jean's decision was wisely taken. By vinifying separately these grapes so laden with sugar and glycerine, he not only allowed himself the luxury of experimenting with unfamiliar techniques (advised by friends in Alsace and Bordeaux), but he ensured that his basic Mâcon, made from the remainder of the crop, was a better-balanced, more elegant, white burgundy than it would otherwise have been. It was typical of a grower who is the most innovative of his region, and who treats the production of Mâcon-Clessé (a decent but modest appellation) with as much seriousness as the most renowned wine-makers of the Côte d'Or. As a result of the care and intelligence with which it is produced, his wine does indeed taste, not infrequently, like a good Meursault.

The *cuvée spéciale*, however, resembles an experiment by Mondavi in California rather than anything that we know from Burgundy. I asked Jean whether it had caused major problems of vinification. 'No, everything went well. I kept the temperature low, and the fermentation continued slowly but steadily, and then stopped by itself at just under fifteen degrees of alcohol, leaving about seventy-five grammes of residual sugar. I didn't allow the malolactic to happen because I wanted to preserve a good level of acidity. But I lost my hair a bit!'

This serious air and quiet, technical approach is enlivened by a smile that flashes across his face, and recalls the schoolboy's toothy grin that you remember from family photographs. His grin is mirrored in the expression of Clothilde and Estelle, his two young daughters, and of Florent and Gauthier, his sons.

He is a man of slight build and modest demeanour who, nevertheless, manages to wear his invariable jeans and windcheater with a certain style, like a tall jockey. There is nothing of the Burgundian in his speech or appearance, so I asked him whether his family had originated in these parts. 'Oh no,' he said. 'We come from the north.' It was this remark that revealed how much he had in common with the strong sense of locality that characterizes the wine-growers of Burgundy, for it transpired that this distant 'north' (which I had visualized as the bleak mining region towards Calais) was actually twenty miles away. His ancestors have always been either *vignerons* (wine-growers) or stonemasons, and his grandfather came from the Charolais but married a girl from Quintaine. After his death she returned with their son (Jean's father) to her native village.

Thévenet has been building an elaborate stone gateway to his house as long as I have known him, but it is the *vigneron*'s heritage, rather than the mason's, that attracts him. The gate remains unfinished because the business of wine-making absorbs all his time and energy.

He has his seven hectares of vineyard at Quintaine on well-drained limestone slopes above his house, within the appellation of Mâcon-Clessé. The vines average between thirty and forty years of age; all are Chardonnay with the exception of a few rows of Gamay, from which Jean makes a little red wine for his own amusement. The advantages of a good site and old vines are considerable, and Jean works hard to maintain the highest standards of cultivation. The work is a repetitive cycle but there are occasional opportunities to try something new. He tested a mechanical harvester recently, but found that the juice went everywhere, and he was worried that the weight of the machine would crush the soil. So he went back to a team of fifteen or more pickers composed of '*un Anglais et beaucoup de Charolais*!' For the rest of the year, he employs two men to help with the cultivation of the vineyard, but reserves to himself alone the entire work of the cellar.

This is where his enthusiasm lies, because the problems of vinification give him endless opportunities to experiment. Unlike so many of his neighbours, who follow, without thinking, the traditional ways, Thévenet is always seeking to improve. He is a committed advocate of technological progress.

Once picked, the grapes are put into small boxes so that they are not crushed but arrive whole, unbroken and unoxidized. The pressing is of critical importance. Pressure that is too violent or too abrupt produces juice that is extremely cloudy, with a great deal of solid matter in suspension. Thévenet is one of the very few growers of his region to have invested in the expensive, but impeccable, Bucher pneumatic press from Switzerland. The results are seen after the *débourbage*, the period of settling and clarification of the juice prior to fermentation. Wishing only to ferment perfectly clear juice, Thévenet was having to discard 20 per cent of cloudy sediment from the bottom of the tank. Since using the new press he has reduced his loss to 7 or 8 per cent. Other growers would ferment the lot, producing a coarser wine.

The major effort, however, is directed towards temperature control. In the old days in the Côte d'Or (though rarely in the Mâconnais), the must was fermented in small oak barrels which allowed for a rapid dispersal of the heat of the yeast's activity and resulted in a slow, low-temperature vinification that could last for up to three months. It is this pattern that Thévenet tries to emulate with modern refrigeration equipment, and a mixture of stainless steel vats and large oak casks. He controls the temperature to between 12 and 17°C, much lower than most would consider wise and only allows it to climb to 19°C then he wishes the malolactic fermentation to start. It is a difficult technique and there is always the danger that he will end up with vinegar rather than wine. It requires impeccable cleanliness especially if (like Thévenet) you are sparing in the use of sulphur, the traditional sterilant.

All of this would be routine in a large, well-equipped California winery, but it is rare indeed in a small grower's cellar in France. The result of this care, however, is a Mâcon that has retained the fresh complexity of aroma, the concentrated elegance of flavour that you look for in fine white burgundy. Like a wine of higher appellation, it needs time to reveal its potential, blossoming to unexpected opulence after eighteen months in bottle.

It can, indeed, last a good deal longer. I remember one evening with Jean and Marie-Thérèse when I called with Tim Marshall, the English broker based at Nuits-St-Georges, who handles all of Thévenet's export sales. We were sitting round a table covered with bottles and glasses and with plates of home-made charcuterie, an onion tart and a bowl of salad. We watched the sun set over the vines, and were serenaded and kissed by the Thévenet daughters on their way to bed. Then we worked our way back through the vintages. The spicy, aromatic richness of the '79 was followed by the leaner, more elegant '78. A surprisingly attractive '77 proved, yet again, that a dedicated *vigneron* can make good wine even in a poor vintage. Then we came to the '62, made by Jean's father. Despite its age this was still lively and fresh with a ripe, mouthfilling intensity. It is said that Mâcon is best drunk young, but here was a twenty-year-old bottle that showed not the slightest sign of decay, and seemed instead to be still improving.

Not every vintage will last so well, and you need heroic patience and self-denial to keep for a generation a wine that will be wholly delicious in a couple of years. Jean himself has few old bottles. He may make the best white Mâcon in the world, but he knows that it is a wine for drinking, not hoarding.

Pierre Cogny

Bouzeron (lovely name for a wine village) is one of those places that always appear half-asleep, with most of the houses firmly shuttered, and neither of the two cafés doing a great deal of business. This is perhaps just as well, since the *pissotière* has an uncomfortably exposed position on the edge of the central square. It is a rusty, green-painted structure that makes minimal concessions to modesty, but its solitary occupant, a large English wine merchant, need have no fear of the stares of the populace. There is no one around.

We are in the Côte Chalonnaise, a somewhat neglected stretch of vineyard between Mâcon and Meursault. Wines like Rully, Givry and Montagny have less renown than Nuits-St-Georges or Vosne-Romanée, but can be excellent and are often bargains. It is a region worth exploring.

Anthony Sarjeant emerges from the Bouzeron convenience. He is one of those odd, indefinable characters in the wine trade who, unlikely as it may seem when you meet them, act as the glue which holds together all manner of deals and connections. Once a power in the export trade to the States, running the legendary New York importers, Frederick Wildman & Sons, Anthony no longer commutes fortnightly across the Atlantic, but moves around Europe in a car that is much too small for him, carrying his basket of samples from *bodega*, *cave* and *cantina* to the country wine merchants of England. He has the air of a man struggling to hold together the impossibly dispersed elements of his life, with his family in England, a house in the Médoc, and his files in the boot of his car.

It was Anthony who originally introduced me to the grower we were about to visit, following a recommendation from his friend the mayor of Bouzeron, Aubert de Villaine. The chain of connections goes back a long way, for Aubert is co-proprietor of the Domaine de la Romanée-Conti, producing some of the world's most coveted wines, which were formerly distributed in the States by Wildman, Sarjeant's erstwhile employer. The wine trade is a very personal business.

We cross the square to knock on a barn door, above which hangs a small sign with the words '*Pierre Cogny, sans intermédiaire sur votre table*'.

Cogny is on his way back from the vineyards and he arrives in a rush. The words of welcome come tumbling out, coated with as thick a Burgundian accent as you could find anywhere. He is a small man, a bit like an extremely vigorous imp; emphatic and enthusiastic; an honest man with a highly developed sense of honour. He makes wonderful wine.

The way through the barn is encumbered by a big pile of woodchips and strips of bark. A boy is busy trimming acacia posts for the vineyard. He works beneath an enormous mask of Tutankhamun, made by Cogny's father-in-law for a village fête, long ago. Besides him is an expensive Vaslin wine-press, carefully sheathed in polythene against the dust. We pick our way through the debris to the cellar. I keep my hat on to protect me from electric shocks. The place is lit by the primitive system, so common in French cellars, of two bare wires, spanned at intervals by devices like inverted clothes-hangers, from which dangle flickering bulbs. The wires are well above Cogny's head, but I have to duck continuously and am not much reassured when he tells me that the voltage is now reduced by a transformer, following a near-fatal accident some years ago.

A local policeman arrives, a friendly fellow with a plump Burgundian belly. He has come to collect some wine but is happy to join us in an extended tasting. Cogny darts about, drawing samples from casks of varying size and indeterminate age, while entertaining us with a non-stop rattle of half-intelligible argot: comments on the wines; folklore about vinification; stories of the past.

There was never enough money when Pierre was young; so he worked for ten years as a railwayman, tramping thirty kilometres a day up and down the lines between Chagny and Puligny, checking the alignment of the rails and cleaning the points. In the evenings and weekends he laboured in his grandfather's vineyards.

In 1963 he was courting. It was one of the wettest years of the decade, and his grandfather was continually urging him back into the vineyard to spray the vines against the rot. The day came when the charms of courtship proved more alluring than this ceaseless toil and Cogny abandoned his task. That night it rained and the downpour continued for two days. They lost the entire crop. It was, says Pierre, a hard lesson.

Marriage added the vineyards of his father-in-law to those inherited from his grandfather. Cogny gave up the railways and concentrated on his little domaine. He has ten hectares all together (about twenty-five acres). Over half is planted with Aligoté, a grape that normally makes a rather astringent, acidic wine, but which flourishes in this region. Cogny's Aligoté is the best I know, with an intensity, a rich spiciness that he attributes to the exceptional age of the vines. It is rare to find Aligoté that has been planted longer than thirty or forty years because the yield decreases significantly beyond this point. Cogny's vines are twice that age.

It is also a matter of vinification. 'If it's a good year, it has good lees* and I like to leave it on its lees for as long as possible.' Timing is important. 'You can't bottle a wine when there's fog, when it's raining or when there's a full moon.'

Such dictates are enunciated with absolute faith, in the same emphatic way that Cogny explains his abhorrence of oxidation, which leads him to top up every cask and *cuve* first thing each morning, replacing the tiny quantity of wine lost by evaporation. He

* The deposit left by wine as it ferments.

hates filtration and cold-stabilization. 'It is absolutely necessary to have a deposit in wine. It is natural and essential for the maturing of wine in bottles. There is no more *vin de garde* [wine to lay down] these days because it is massacred at birth.'

Most people regard Aligoté as a wine for rapid consumption, but Cogny knows that it can last indefinitely. 'My grandfather kept some Aligoté from the year of my mother's birth. He protected the cork with wax. The wine, though oxidized on the nose, was still good on the palate.'

Cogny also makes Rully, both white and red. The white is from Pinot Blanc, a variety that has mostly been replaced by Chardonnay, but which can produce classic white burgundy. We taste three samples of the 1983. The first is tremendous: high in alcohol and rich in flavour (typical of the year) but none the less spicy and elegant, with great length of flavour. The second cask is finer still, a wine of extraordinary concentration. *'C'essxtra!'* says Cogny. The third sample is from the cask nearest the door. It is cloudy and unsettled. 'That cask is always the slowest. It catches the draught. But none of these wines is really ready for tasting yet. You will have to wait for Easter.'

There is no one quite like Cogny. I love visiting him for his wine, for the stories he tells and the traditions that he embodies. Most of all, I love the fact that he is one of those rare people who never says anything for effect. His life is seamless. His words leap from the heart.

Aubert de Villaine

Diagonally across the square from Cogny's cellars in Bouzeron is located the house of the mayor, Aubert de Villaine. For a man who is co-proprietor of the Domaine de la Romanée-Conti (the most renowned estate of the Côte d'Or) the house has a modest exterior but, in typical Burgundian fashion, its façade is deceptive, concealing a courtyard, garden and spacious *cuverie*. A comparable trick is played by Aubert himself. A pair of muddy boots and well-worn jeans, a shapeless pullover with holes at the elbows, a large pair of spectacles and a cap bought on a fishing holiday in Ireland clothe, with a diffident air, the lean frame of a highly intelligent man, one of the very few growers of Burgundy to have a cosmopolitan understanding of the world. His wife, Pamela, is American, and their friends and interests are international. But no one would doubt that, however much he may appear the studious intellectual, Aubert is at heart a countryman, engrossed in his locality and in the business of making wine.

He and Pamela settled in Bouzeron after their marriage, and it is here that they cultivate twenty hectares of vines. The estate may be less renowned than the Domaine de la Romanée-Conti, but it gives Aubert a chance to be entirely his own master – something that is not possible at the DRC itself, where decisions are the joint responsibility of several very different personalities. Madame Bize-Leroy, who shares with Aubert and his father the ownership of the Domaine, has an extremely forceful character, while de Villaine senior is somewhat retiring. Then there is the large figure of André Noblet to consider, firmly ensconced as *régisseur* (manager) since thirty years or more. Clearly there are conflicts, of partnership and generation, but this is a subject on which Aubert is reticent in the extreme. One senses a man biding his time who, for the present, is glad to create his own reputation at Bouzeron, without benefit of famous site or centuries of accumulated traditions.

The atmosphere at vintage time certainly has a lively informality. Entering the courtyard in 1982, just before midday, I was greeted by a small army of pickers, cellar-workers and friends who were bringing in the last grapes of an abundant vintage. It was a busy and cheerful scene, for all was going well and it was getting close to lunchtime. For over a fortnight Pamela had been feeding thirty-five people a day, and delicious smells of cooking drifted from the house to mingle with the aroma of fermenting wine.

The scene in the cellars was of barely controlled pandemonium, for this was a harvest of unprecedented size. A friend of Aubert's from Paris, director of an international firm of head-hunters, was helping to oversee the vinification, endeavouring to find space for the mass of healthy grapes.

Aubert told me that the problem was general throughout the region, and that fermentation space was at such a premium that some growers were driven to desperate measures. Many had filled their bathtubs, and one had even resorted to hijacking. Apparently one man from the Côte d'Or had ordered new *cuves* from a manufacturer in the south. The driver of the low-loader on which they were being transported had stopped to relieve himself in a lay-by in the Beaujolais. A quickwitted grower rushed up to him with a fistful of thousand-franc notes. 'Those tanks are mine,' he said. 'Follow me.' The driver pocketed the money and obediently delivered his load at the nearby cellars. By the time the original consignee had discovered their whereabouts, the *cuves* were full of fermenting Beaujolais.

Aubert himself had to empty two vats of red burgundy after a week to make room for a fresh load of grapes, though he normally allows the fermentation to continue undisturbed for between twelve and fifteen days, treading and plunging down the *chapeau* (the cap of skins and pulp) three or four times a day, to get the maximum extract of colour and tannin. As for the whites, the juice was so abundant that he used only the first pressing. He was delighted with the quality. 'A really good year for white burgundy and the reds will be most agreeable, though they will not be wines for long keeping.'

He makes Aligoté, Chardonnay and Pinot Noir. The Aligoté de Bouzeron is generally considered superior to the Aligoté from other regions of Burgundy, and Aubert is proud of the part that he has played in re-establishing its reputation. His is certainly attractive, without the harsh acidity that is associated with this grape. Partly it is a matter of controlled, low-temperature vinification (though not as low as Thévenet), and partly the fact that this modest wine is very grandly housed: a third of the harvest is matured in casks that have previously done a season or two at the Domaine de la Romanée-Conti. On the end of each barrel is stencilled the word 'Montrachet'.

Aubert's Bourgogne Les Clous, pure Chardonnay, gets the same treatment though a higher proportion is matured in cask. It has the reserved elegance of classic white burgundy when young, needing a year or two in bottle to show its true character. It never develops the opulent, buttery character of Thévenet's Mâcon, but matures into a miniature Puligny rather than a miniature Meursault.

Aubert's best *cuvée* of red is called La Digoine. It is classic Pinot Noir, with firmness of structure from the old vines, and supple charm from the more recent replantings (the same clonal selection as is used at the Romanée-Conti). This wine, too, is matured in second-hand casks from the Domaine, most of them marked 'La Tache', though de Villaine does use a few new casks each year to give extra tannin and a hint of oak.

The cellars descend three storeys down the slope of a hill. They are cold and extremely humid, excellent for the wine but less good for humans. After tasting numerous samples of the past couple of vintages, from cask, *cuve* and bottle, it was a relief to re-emerge into the courtyard and head back towards the warmth of the kitchen. The team of pickers had already sat down, and we squeezed on to the benches beside them. They were a very mixed bunch, including men and women from the village who come every year, and others from further afield who were here for the first time. There was even a student from Japan. They had been working together for over a fortnight and had become good friends. One of the girls was a tease, and one of the men had the lugubrious mobile face that is the mark of the French clown. These two characters were the poles of a great deal of noise, joking and laughter which increased as the meal progressed. There was plenty of wine and the food was delicious.

Eventually lunch was over and everyone piled out of the house again, well fed and red-faced. The pickers formed a slightly drunken chorus line and danced across the square for our entertainment. Back in the vineyards, however, anarchy gave way to discipline as they returned to work with surprising energy. Aubert was there, ensuring that no rotten or green grapes were picked, hurrying them on to finish gathering the vintage before the rain came, for the sky was clouding over and the air felt wet.

It is this attention to detail, the personal supervision of every important task, that sets the good growers apart from the rest. They will discuss their theories of vinification or argue about clonal selection, but each will express a different and equally convincing point of view. The common factor is an enthusiasm that never allows the grower to treat the daily tasks as a matter of routine. It is Thévenet's mania for cleanliness, Cogny's insistence on topping up his casks each morning, and de Villaine's capacity to enthuse his workers that result, finally, in the superior quality of their wines.

Sometimes this pursuit of perfection can verge on fanaticism. Aubert told me that in 1983 the vineyards at the Domaine de la Romanée-Conti had been struck by hail. In order to eliminate the unpleasant taste of damaged berries from that year's wine they had sent out the vineyard workers armed with tweezers. For most of August and much of September they had picked out, grape by grape, the hail-struck fruit. It is actions like this that help to justify the otherwise indefensible price of the final product.

Aubert told me this story as we were tasting his own wines in the cellars at Bouzeron on a cold morning in February. I had brought my family to lunch, intending to question him closely on the problems of price and quality in relation to the Domaine. But this was the closest I got to an answer that day, and the warmth of Aubert and Pamela's hospitality deterred me from my purpose. Back at the house I found our daughter, Hana, playing with Ibis, the tolerant dog, in front of a blazing fire, while Irène chatted to Pamela in the kitchen. Anthony Sarjeant and Aubert began reminiscing about Freddie Wildman who had just announced his re-entry to the wine trade after some years in the pursuit of architecture. The conversation moved to and fro across the Atlantic, from wine to music via politics, and it was not until the apple pudding that I returned to the attack, with a few provocative remarks about the marketing of Romanée-Conti wines.

Aubert listened with courtesy but yielded no indiscretions. He was more interested in talking about the progress they were making at Bouzeron, and the way that this reflected what was, in his view, a huge increase in quality in Burgundy in recent years. 'Burgundy is still the stained-glass window that it was twenty years ago, a fragmented pattern of small-holdings. But in addition to the well-established domaines, there are a lot of new growers worth following; men like Michelot in Nuits-St-Georges, Jayer in Vosne-Romanée, Coche-Dury at Meursault. Or *"le petit Cogny"* across the road. These men justify Burgundy's reputation for quality and give one hope for the future.'

This indeed is my experience; that the renown of the classic regions is not built solely on accidents of soil and climate, but on the continuing resilience of a human tradition.

III
Scenes of Village Life: Meursault

A Day at the Paulée

The term '*la Paulée*' is of disputed origin, but it is generally agreed that it means a vintage feast, harvest-home. La Paulée de Meursault is the last of three such feasts, '*Les Trois Glorieuses*', that surround the annual auction of wines at the Hospices de Beaune. It is the most exclusive and the greatest fun.

It has a number of unique features that contribute to its holding a legendary place in the mythology of wine-lovers and gourmets. In the first place, it is a genuine village affair, with admission confined to the growers of Meursault and a few friends. There is little room for outsiders. The second distinction of the Paulée is that, unlike the other great feasts of this long November weekend, it is a lunchtime affair, with the result that everyone is less formally dressed, more at ease and has greater stamina! Finally, there is the most unusual element of all. As the menu says, alongside the list of six mouth-watering courses: '*Selon tradition . . . chacun apporte sa bouteille.*'* For this is the greatest of all bottle parties – a feast at which the growers vie with one another to produce rarities from their private cellars. At the 1979 Paulée, at the table dominated by André Ropiteau and his friends, this central tradition of the feast resulted in the fortunate guests consuming one of the most dazzling arrays of fine burgundies ever offered at a single meal. There *are* moments of self-indulgence in the wine trade. This was one of them.

* As is traditional . . . everyone brings his own bottle.

After a morning spent tasting wine with Robert Drouhin, and sampling mustard with Monsieur Desfossey, I arrived at Meursault at midday to be greeted by André with a grin that suggested he was prepared to overlook my criticism of one of his wines a couple of days earlier. He strode across the courtyard of Ropiteau Frères to his private cellars next door, and filled a wicker basket with some extremely ancient-looking bottles, the name and vintage chalked on their unlabelled sides. More guests appeared: a couple of English wine merchants arrived from a large tasting at Remoissenet, while Jean-Pierre Nié and Russell Hone of Les Fils de Marcel Quancard came bearing another hoard of dusty treasures. An Anglo-Swiss broker of luxuries to the very rich arrived, together with a naval dentist with their respective girl friends, as Anne Ropiteau drove up looking breathless. We stood around, stamping our feet and breathing steam into the cold air of a bright November day. There was a sense of expectation; it felt like Christmas. The gendarmes of Meursault were in their best uniforms, and looked amiably red-faced, while the chefs occasionally emerged into the street from their labours, equally red-faced but harassed. The streets were full of wine-growers in their Sunday best, and the village was *en fête*. We strode up the road to the Paulée.

There appeared to be no formal start to the banquet: the first bottle was opened as soon as we fought our way through the crowd at the door and found our places. It was a wine from the extraordinary trove amassed by the wholesaler Vanier (and acquired after his death by the house of Quancard), a 1959 Meursault. Already we were tasting something of remarkable quality: golden, honeyed but dry, concentrated and long on the palate. Guests were still entering the hall, and the mayor had yet to make his speech of welcome, but the second bottle was opened. This, another Vanier/Quancard treasure, was a 1929 Montagny. It was sensational: hard to believe that at fifty years of age a wine from this relatively unknown appellation could display such youthful concentration of flavour. Brilliant; golden; the colour indicated a wine still unmarked by oxidation. Less assertive than the preceding Meursault, the Montagny had a gentle, enchanting complexity of flavour which clothed extraordinary intensity and length. It was a wine to which I returned again and again over the next hour or so. It showed no signs of fading and dominated every wine that followed.

Following a brief and well-phrased welcome from the mayor, the first course arrived: quails, boned and stuffed with two varieties of foie gras, a bird for each of the 359 guests. These delicious morsels, requiring such infinite patience to prepare and eaten with such rapidity, were washed down by a couple more Meursaults from the Quancard cellar. The first was a curious 1933 which had a pronounced smell of apricots, like a Tokay Szamorodni (the dry version of the famous sweet Hungarian wine, Tokay Aszu). The second, a 1947 Premier Cru, was corky.

In the ensuing pause between courses, André began opening wine from the Ropiteau domaine, starting with a straight 1959 Meursault and following with an outstanding Meursault Poruzots of the same vintage. This was a wonderful wine, still retaining a lively acidity. Fresh, youthful and elegant, it looked well set-up for at least another decade. We drank it while listening to the speech of introduction for the winner of the *Prix de la Paulée*, awarded annually to a writer who has concerned himself with some aspect of Bourgignon life. Jean d'Ormesson, France's youngest Academician, was the recipient. He is a writer who has particularly endeared himself to the village of Meursault by authorizing the introduction of the word *'Paulée'* into the official French Dictionary. Publication of the relevant volume was still some way in the future since the French Academy had only just completed work on the letter 'E', but Monsieur d'Ormesson promised to fill the interval enjoying his prize (of a hundred bottles of Meursault) in the company of the prettiest young girls of his acquaintance.

It was a very French speech. Witty and urbane, articulating with extraordinary clarity and an elegance of language and style all the more impressive for the absence of notes, the Academician entranced his audience. The only trouble was that he continued ten minutes longer than was necessary to allow the paupiettes of sole cardinal to be served in perfect condition.

A Meursault Genevrières of the 1977 vintage was sent down the table from another party, but met with a cool response, since it smelled and tasted of brown sauce. André produced his own Genevrières of the 1959 vintage and no one quibbled. It was a big, fat wine at the height of its maturity.

The first red wine followed. It was, inevitably, a wine from André's home village of Monthélie and born in the same year as him: 1947. Although not a great classic, this was a wine that could easily have passed as twenty years younger. It contrasted well with a

1970 Monthélie from Moillard that we were offered by a neighbour. White wines were still appearing from different directions: a 1957 Meursault Poruzots of Bernard Thevenot (better on nose than palate) and a 1970 Meursault Perrières of Michelot Garnier which started well but was a little short. Meanwhile, the third course appeared: a delicate Ratafia sauce in which truffles swam leisurely around breast of chicken. A 1969 Pommard Chanlains from André's cellar was showing its age, but the Quancard party had started opening bottles again, and we were building up to a competitive finale.

The food kept coming: huge joints of Charolais beef were borne shoulder-high into the hall, and somehow everyone was served with a perfectly cooked portion, pink and tender, with beans and carrots almost equally *à point*. A miracle of village catering. This course, and the cheese that followed, was offset by three sensational wines.

A 1934 Romanée St Vivant from the Quancard stable set the pace. By any standards this was extraordinary. The colour was still deep and it had the bouquet of a fine Pomerol. Amazingly youthful, its soft immediacy was backed by remarkable depth and length of flavour. Jean-Pierre Nié and Russell Hone then produced their star – a 1921 Clos Vougeot. The colour was still strong, but showing that delicacy at the edges which is typical of a fine old wine. It smelled wonderful; a complex aroma of mushrooms and the sweet fragrance of the pinot grape. Finesse had replaced force, with layer upon delicate layer of flavour.

André, however, still had something in reserve. With uncharacteristic reticence he poured his last bottle, a 1928 Bonnes Mares. The wine instantly dominated the conversation. The colour was impressive, exceptionally deep for a wine of this age, and the scent was rich, powerful and classically pinot. An immediate fear that it might be drying out on the palate was succeeded by appreciation of the weight of fruit, and the flavour which persisted behind the residual mask of tannin. Too elusive to analyse, the wine combined something of rose petals and blackberries. It was as clearly the finest of the red wines we had tasted as the 1929 Montagny was of the whites.

Honours, finally, were even, with superb wines from both camps enjoyed by seriously appreciative guests. The rest was light relief: a 1971 Clos de la Roche from Antonin Rodet appeared from a neighbour and received a rather patronizing welcome, while the

1974 Gevrey Chambertin that crept in from Jaboulet Vercherre was left almost untasted. To finish, however, we enjoyed the unusual combination of a vigorous eau-de-vie of Poire William, distilled by a local grower, and a customs cask sample of five-year-old Longmorn Glenlivet at 110° proof, smuggled in by Ken Ingleton. Together with strong coffee, they fortified us for the ordeal to come.

For the Meursault Paulée does not finish with the end of the meal, five hours after sitting down at the table. On the contrary, this extraordinary feast is merely the prologue to a test of stamina by which the growers of Meursault separate the men from the boys amongst the connoisseurs of their beloved wines. In the following three and a half hours we tasted and discussed a further fifteen young Meursaults and assorted other wines and spirits, progressing from one small cellar to another. The day, it appeared, had just begun.

After appraising the previous two vintages of most of the major growths of Meursault, we ended with a few older wines, culminating in a fine 1972 Echezeaux. Finally it was time to visit André's latest baby – a small cellar devoted to the maturation, in new oak casks, of unblended vintages of eau-de-vie and Marc de Bourgogne. The intention is that they shall be bottled at natural strength from the year 2000. We ended with a 1974 Fine, beginning to round out, but still a raw, invigorating taste to set us on our way to the culminating event of the day's programme: a great party at the Moulin aux Moines.

Every year for the previous twenty, Madame Thévenin had invited the guests of the Paulée to eat, drink and dance at her spectacular eighteenth-century mill. The enormous rooms were crowded with the entire population of Meursault, each greeted at the door by Madame – a small upright figure, icon-like in white.

Log fires, bread and cheese, and jugs of the new Beaujolais were hugely welcome. By midnight it was like the aftermath of a marathon, as the village celebrated the end of an extraordinary day.

As André said at one late stage of the evening: 'You know, *la Paulée*, it's a pleasure, but it's work too!'

André Ropiteau, Wild Man

For twelve generations there have been Ropiteaus in and around the village of Meursault. Some were eccentric, most were connected with wine, and almost all of them looked remarkably similar – a likeness that has been inherited by André Ropiteau. *'De père en fils depuis 1593,'* it says on his card.

Sometimes I worry about inbreeding, particularly in country villages. André is my age (thirty-eight at the time of writing), and he is a wild man; a cunning Burgundian with the exuberant madness of some of those Dubliners that you used to encounter in the back bar of Jamet's during holy hour in Horse Show week.

'I'm crazee you know! It's very important to be crazy in life. It's important to do what the others are not doing.'

André's father was a lawyer in Dijon who took no great interest in the family wine business until his brother was killed in 1940. He took charge at a difficult time, but continued to develop the firm of Ropiteau Frères, both as *négociants* (buying wine from other growers in the region), and as agents for the family domaine of Ropiteau-Mignon. In 1965, however, he sold the company to Chantovent (big distributors of table wine and *vin de pays*). The contract included, amongst other things, an agreement for Ropiteau Frères to pur-chase the entire crop of the family vineyards for the next twenty-one years, until 1986.

So the father stopped working and spent more and more time in his library, an amazing two-storey room with books lining the walls, books covering every desk and table and books piled in precarious heaps on the floor. The collection originated with a printing and publishing business owned by a nineteenth-century Ropiteau, and grew as various members of the family cleared out their bookcases and packed off the unwanted volumes to old man Ropiteau's house in Meursault.

André himself is no intellectual ('I wasn't good at school. I made no studies at all'), but equally there is no one less suited to working in a large organization. Neither the library nor the new group of Ropiteau Frères and Chantovent could occupy his interest for long.

He went to London to learn his own, highly idiosyncratic version of English and (in the unlikely setting of the Centre Charles Peguy, the French youth centre in Leicester Square) he met his future wife, a girl from St Jean de Luz. André returned to France in 1969, and spent a few months working for Domaines Ott in Provence before marrying Anne and going home to the village of Monthélie, where he was born.

'At that time taking care of the vineyards was for the stupid of the family! When I came back to Burgundy in 1970 I looked for an unplantable piece of land that still had the appellation.'

He pored over maps and criss-crossed the vineyards until he found what he was searching for: a long strip on the north-east edge of the *premier cru* vineyard of Puligny Chamuleaux, a strip that lay alongside the boundary with Meursault. It was uncultivated for the very good reason that it was a rocky outcrop covered with stones; a vast heap that had piled up over the centuries as the surrounding vineyards were cleared and planted. He bought this patch for 80,000 francs (about £6,000): 'They thought I was crazy.'

André, however, knew a contractor. A thousand lorry-loads of unwanted stones from the hill above Puligny were carted away for nothing, and ended up as a bridge in front of the railway station at Chalon. A few loads of soil were brought back to give the vines a foothold. After the inevitable battle with the authorities, André won the right to the *premier cru* appellation. His hectare of rock is now worth thirty times what he paid for it and produces about 6,000 bottles a year of marvellous white burgundy. 'I am a builder, I like to create,' he says.

In similar fashion, André has gradually extended his domaine to over ten hectares. His biggest vineyard dominates a hillside that can be seen from the garden of his house in Monthélie. By studying old maps he discovered that an uncultivated patchwork of wilderness had, 200 years ago, formed a single walled vineyard of six hectares. It had been abandoned because the slopes were steep and the work was hard, but he reasoned that modern tractors could overcome these difficulties and set to work to acquire the land. There were forty-seven different owners, and it took him ten years of patience and guile. 'You 'ave to be *malin* [a cunning devil],' says André.

He showed me the vines at a wet and miserable time of the year, driving along rutted tracks, fighting for traction between the potholes. When we finally came down from the slopes above Monthélie, the car was covered with red mud, the tyres had lost several millimetres of tread and my notes were illegible. André, however, was in full flow.

'I want to speak and to become known my village Monthélie – it's very small, only eighty hectares [200 acres] – but all the vineyards is hills, makes very elegant, very sophisticated wine, like the *nouvelle cuisine* I like.

'New style for me means delicate wine, sophisticated wine with aromas, finesse. People don't want to be heavy after drinking wine. For example, me, I prefer Monthélie to Pommard – and people want white wines more now.

'The people from Bordeaux are more professionals, cleverer than Burgundians. In Burgundy we work too much with the tradition. I say that because I am not traditional. I think it is very, very important to do new ways. Example, about fertilization. The people put every time the same things. They don't look inside the body of the earth. But the young people are taking much more care. They want to be cleverer and think about what they do. But we also have more power now with the new machines. It is important for making the best wines to plant the best plants. People are planting the clones.'

André's latest projects are centred on an old house in Meursault which he intends to convert into a restaurant. Below the house are fine, fifteenth-century cellars in which he matures the wine from his own vineyards and, in a wing at the back, he has installed a gleaming new storage and bottling plant. In another wing are André's offices.

We are greeted, with an air of extraordinary flamboyance, by Bernard: retired commissioner of police; Latin scholar; owner of a tremendous moustache and a Burgundian belly; lover of old buildings.

'They call him Clemenceau round here,' whispers André mysteriously, as the old man discusses the work that he is doing, ripping down modern ceilings and partitions to reveal the fine beams and original structure of the house.

'Clemenceau' departs, swaying gently on his bicycle, and we walk down the street to taste a few casks of vintage marc and eau-de-vie in another cellar, before driving off to see Bernard Michelot, president of the Meursault growers' association. André has a court case to discuss, another of his long-drawn-out battles with the authorities.

It seems that during the 1982 vintage the *'gabelous'* came to Meursault. The term is medieval slang for 'salt-taxers', and refers to the widely disliked inspectors of indirect taxes. They wanted to check sugar stocks in the cellars but everyone was so busy that, led by Michelot, all the growers refused them admission.

A short while later they returned, accompanied by gendarmes from Dijon (who are not normally allowed to work in the region of Beaune). As the result, it is said, of a denunciation by a disgruntled ex-employee of Ropiteau, they headed straight for André's cellars. A cellarman came running to warn him while he was snatching a quick lunch at his mother's house. The inspectors were already in the cellars (this is illegal, except in the owner's presence), so André telephoned Michelot who alerted his fellow growers. About twenty of them assembled at the Ropiteau *cuverie* and effectively ejected the inspectors from the premises. 'They had to leave because otherwise their car would be on the roof, the wheels in the sky!' There was a great row which resulted in Ropiteau and Michelot ending up in court, charged with obstruction of justice. Of course they were guilty technically, but the opinion of the court on the matter was expressed by purely token fines.

The authorities were so incensed that they appealed, demanding much stiffer penalties, and the matter is about to come once more before the courts. Ropiteau and Michelot have to co-ordinate their defence. It is a case which is destined to drag on for many months to come.

By the time we return to the office in Meursault it is six o'clock – the perfect moment, it seems, to taste everything in the cellar. But first there is a telex to deal with (some Corton Charlemagne is needed), and a telephone call regarding a large consignment of wines for export. André beams: 'I am very 'appy with that. It's a lot of money. A lot!'

A woman comes in, looking for a job in the vineyards, and swaps village gossip with André while he issues instructions to his assistant.

In the cellars we taste twenty casks (*pièces*) of wine from the last two vintages. I particularly like one *pièce* of Chambolle-Musigny and, having agreed a price, I buy it on the spot. At André's insistence I chalk my name on the cask. Loftus his mark. Then we taste another fifteen wines, older vintages, and I buy a few cases from the family reserves.

It is eight o'clock and I am beginning to flag, but André decides to telephone Texas. 'Yess. It eez André Ropiteau 'phoning from France.' There is a gabble at the other end and André covers the mouthpiece with his hand. 'Oh that Tegsas agsent. Imposseebal to understand!'

Finally we return home, having dissuaded André from driving forty miles to dinner at his favourite restaurant at Saulieu. In the kitchen at Monthélie, Irène is giving Hana her supper while Fanny

Ropiteau practises her English and her brother Remi struggles with his homework. Anne, with a relaxed but somewhat distracted air, is cooking dinner. In this atmosphere of relative calm André, at last, slows down.

During the meal we drink Meursault and Monthélie. We talk about André's career as a film star (he has a small part in a rural drama called *Le destin de Juliette*) and we discuss Anne's hopes for an exhibition in Paris of her patchwork collages. Inevitably, the conversation reverts to wine.

'I'm not an intellectual, but I get on very well with sensitive people. Perhaps making wine is similar. You have an idea in the head. It's like the great cooks. You have to think and have it in the head before you do it.'

For the future, André sees a continuing decline in the fortunes of the big companies in Burgundy and sees everyone, growers and *négociants* alike, concentrating on their own village, their own specialized patch. He himself is selling the little vineyard in Chambolle-Musigny which produced the wine that I had bought earlier. It is fifty kilometres away, too far to bother about.

'I stick to Meursault now. I am child of Meursault.'

The next morning we have a leisurely breakfast with Anne, while André rushes to Dijon to see his lawyer. He returns just as we are setting off for the airport, grinning with delight.

'*Une vedette américaine* will be tried in court tomorrow as well as me. So there will be journalists and photographers from all over France.'

As always, he is full of new plans. 'Come, come! I want to show you something. Look at that little building at the end of the garden. I think last night I will make it a place for friends to stay, make it really nice. It will be ready when you come next time.' And he roars with laughter as he sends us on our way.

IV
Quantity or Quality:
The Choice for Europe

The Wine Lake

The problem is simple: consumption of basic table wine in Europe is on the decline while production continues slowly to increase. The mismatch between demand and supply cannot be corrected without threatening the livelihood of up to 85 per cent of the wine growers of Italy, and a similar proportion of those in the Languedoc-Roussillon area of southern France. In order to prevent the enormous social upheavals that would result from the free play of market forces, the European Economic Community protects these producers of unsaleable rotgut by various measures, including tariffs to inhibit the importation of inexpensive wine from outside the EEC, and the system of 'intervention prices' that has become so notorious an element of EEC agricultural policy. If the 'free' market price falls below a certain level, because of surpluses in production, the EEC will intervene to subsidize the growers, buying up their wine for storage or distillation. The theory is that surplus stocks of wine can be released back on the market in times of shortage, and that the distillate is saleable as industrial alcohol. In practice it is much cheaper to produce alcohol by other means, and no one wants poor wine at any price. Hence the Wine Lake, nearly 500 million gallons deep, costing the Community budget over £400 million per annum.

The fact that production of bad wine continues to increase, despite expensive schemes to grub-up poor-quality vineyards, is evidence that the policy is simply substituting new problems for old. Rather than helping the poor growers to adapt to changing times by switching to other crops, there is evidence that the intervention price is set too high, encouraging vast over-production and wide-scale abuse of the system. Details of the methods adopted in Sicily (where else?) were revealed in 'Foubert's Diary', the gossip column of the English trade magazine, *Wine & Spirit*:

No less than 70 per cent (some say 80) of Sicilian wine production, it seems, finds its way these days into distilleries financed by the European Community (i.e. by you and me). Where are these distilleries? Why, in some cases, right inside the wineries themselves!

There was Foubert, in the heart of the beautiful spaghetti-western countryside, standing in the most superbly equipped modern winery he had ever seen, the capacity of which must have been enormous, judging by the serried ranks of gigantic stainless steel storage and fermentation vessels. Where did the wine come from? From grapes grown in 600 surrounding hectares of *tendone*-trained vineyard, capable of producing 300 hectolitres per hectare (at least)*. Who owned the vineyards and the winery? A couple of brothers, Foubert was told in a tremulous whisper, famous for their 'family' connections. And the whole thing, it seemed, had been financed by 'contributions' from EEC and Sicilian government coffers.

And there, in the adjoining section of the building (although the guided tour did not extend to this part), was the distillation equipment and the enormous storage tanks for the distillate, which the EEC was compelled to buy though no one had any use for it.

Not a bad wheeze, Foubert thought. You get the authorities to finance your vineyards and your winery, employing 'friendly' construction firms and purchasing equipment at top prices from distributors with whom you have 'connections'. You produce feeble grapes at maximum yield, which you turn into undrinkable plonk for which distillation is almost too kind a fate, and you sell the whole lot to the EEC (Foubert was assured that 100 per cent of last year's crop was knocked down to this biggest of buyers) who pay you to convert it to alcohol *and* to store it as *well* as for the produce itself.

'A convenient way of circulating capital', Foubert was informed. Looking around at the scowling, unshaven faces of the chain-smoking 'winemakers' with whom he was sharing Spanish brandy and Scotch whisky (no one offered any wine: presumably there wasn't any), Foubert thought he had better circulate his person right out of that place. Fast.

* This is about six times the production per hectare permitted in Bordeaux.

As can be imagined, the political pressures to preserve a system that benefits so many people are sufficient to indicate continued inertia in the matter of reforming EEC agricultural policy. Nonetheless it is worth considering what might be done, if the political will were there.

There is little hope of persuading people to drink more, at least in the wine-producing countries themselves, where per capita consumption remains remarkably high. The overall decline in the wine market cannot be reversed. But within that market it is clear that there is increasing demand for wine of higher quality, particularly that which has a clear regional or varietal identity.

EEC policy should therefore concentrate on replanting high-yielding, low-grade vines with better quality, lower-yielding varieties. The grower still gets a reasonable return per hectare, because improved quality means a better price, while reduced productivity brings supply back in line with demand. Quality goes up, quantity goes down; both grower and consumer are content.

Of course, this is an expensive policy to implement, but it is the only one that will reduce the long-term financial burden on the EEC Community, while preserving the traditional livelihood of large numbers of European farmers.

The focus of effort must be the co-operatives, the regional associations of local growers. With their teams of technical experts and centralized wine-making facilities, these organizations can both communicate with the individual growers, providing help and technical advice, and ensure that the improvements in viticulture are translated into better wine.

Large numbers of these co-operatives fall well below the ideal standard; dirty, conservative and uninviting, they epitomize the inward-looking incompetence which typifies the regional isolation of so many small growers in France and Italy. There are, however, sufficient exceptions to generate hope for the future. In the well-known appellations you can find a good number of excellent co-ops making wine which sets the standard for their region. The problem, however, lies in the unknown stretches of the vinicultural map; the backwaters where years of depression have bred a habit of resigned mediocrity. It is here that real progress must be made, and it is for this reason that I have chosen to offer one enlightened example of what is possible: the Union de Producteurs Plaimont.

La Gascogne en Bouteille

There is an area of Gascony, north of Pau, that has a particularly invigorating feel: it is a wide rolling landscape rising into steep hills, with the Pyrenees in the distance and vast skies overhead. Here is the land of Armagnac and *foie gras*; of gastronomic traditions that combine great subtlety with down-to-earth peasant directness. There is a tremendous capacity for enjoying the round of seasonal activity. For some the *palombes* (wild pigeons) are everything in life. They are the excuse for spending a great deal of time in the autumn sitting in trees, drinking and singing together, waiting for the flocks of pigeons to come from the south, from the mountainous border with Spain. For others the vintage is the time of celebration. The Plaimont Co-operative refuses to allow mechanical harvesting, partly for technical reasons (they prefer to vinify whole grapes, and they don't think the machines are yet good enough), but also because the harvest is a *fête*, a time when the vineyards should be full of people, working and enjoying themselves together.

The decision to use people rather than machines is typical of André Dubosc, Directeur Général of the Union de Producteurs Plaimont. '*Attention*, God speaks,' they say whenever he opens his mouth. Everyone laughs, but you know that there is affectionate respect for the man who is helping to guide the Co-operative to ever-increasing success. Enthusiastic, youthful, energetic; he has some of the dash of that other local hero, d'Artagnan.

The Union de Producteurs was formed at one of the most difficult moments for the wine trade in general, and for this region in particular. On 1 August 1974 (the day that everyone goes on holiday), the three small co-operatives based in the towns of Aigan, Plaisance and St Mont merged into a single group under the Plaimont banner. Together they controlled 90 per cent of the production of the Côtes de St Mont (authorized as a legally recognized wine region only the previous year), but the general outlook was depressing. Most of their production of red wine was sold in bulk at very low prices to the big blenders of *vin de table*, and much of the white wine was distilled into Armagnac. Sales of both table wine and Armagnac were declining.

They did have one thing in their favour: the inexplicable fact that the average age of the *viticulteurs* was then unusually low. Their president, Monsieur Lescun, is the oldest of them, but he is still only sixty; a vigorous and progressive man. This meant that there was an unusually open-minded attitude to change, quite unlike the die-hard regional chauvinism that typifies many of the viticultural backwaters of France. In most areas it is the young men who have left the land, leaving their fathers and grandfathers to struggle on, tied to their inadequate comprehension of the old traditions.

In this part of Gascony the traditions had almost died. Madiran, the region's only renowned red wine, had virtually ceased to exist at one point, and was only revived by a great deal of hard work during the past generation. Other local wines had been forgotten. 'There were twenty grape varieties specific to this region, and they almost disappeared, especially the whites,' says André Dubosc.

Son of a wine-grower of Madiran, he studied oenology at Bordeaux and viticulture at Montpellier. Further oenological research was followed by a couple of years in Algeria, studying the problems of making decent wine in a hot climate. He returned to Gascony in 1974 with a passion for the history of the vines and vineyards of his region, and he joined the newly formed Union de Producteurs as viticultural technician.

He set to work like an archaeologist tracking down the regional grape varieties, investigating the soil, the microclimate and alternative methods of pruning. 'There is a description of high cultivation here in the eighteenth century; it started near here in the Jurançon.' They used to grow the vines up a rectangular frame, six feet tall and four and a half feet square at its base. Two vines were planted at each corner.

It is often assumed that high cultivation, minimizing the risk of ground frost and giving the vines a better exposure to the sun, is a recent innovation, but there is plenty of evidence that our ancestors recognized its advantages centuries ago. There is a long tradition of its use in Piedmont, while here in Gascony it was clearly developed to allow the grapes to benefit from the late autumn sunshine, without fear of damage from the early morning frost. For August is often wet, and the maturing season stretches out into the long Indian summer that invariably follows. It is not unusual for white grapes to be picked as late as November, or even December. And today they are once more grown to the same height as they were in the eighteenth century, though they are now trained on wires, rather than cumbersome trellises.

All of this Dubosc explains to me, standing in one of the vineyards on a plateau above the wide valley of the Adour. 'We can't plant the vines lower down because the sub-soil is compact, impenetrable clay. They would become waterlogged.' His voice is gentle but insistent, and his sentences pour out with the enthusiasm of a good teacher. These vines are the traditional varieties of the region, rather than the ubiquitous Grenache or Cabernet Sauvignon, Chardonnay or Sauvignon Blanc. Dubosc was determined from the start that they should build on what they had, rather than join the producers of Euro-clone wines. Their motto today is *'La Gascogne en bouteille'.*

This means that they do grow Cabernet, but it is mostly Bouchet (Cabernet Franc) rather than the Cabernet Sauvignon of the Médoc. It is, in any case, subsidiary to Tannat, the principal variety of this region (known as Cot in Cahors, and related to the almost defunct Malbec of Bordeaux). And then there is the wild-sounding Fer Servadou (or Pinenc), a grape that Dubosc values highly for the quality of its aroma.

From these red varieties they produce Madiran, Côtes de St Mont and the basic Côtes de Gascogne. It was on these wines that the Plaimont Co-operative concentrated at first, trying to build a market for wines in bottle rather than relying on bulk sales to the blenders. They established a series of regional tasting centres and shops, selling direct to the public, and slowly built a reputation based on a higher level of quality than was general for such regional wines.

Right from the start they set themselves higher standards. Dubosc helped revitalize the quality of local viticulture, and the Co-operative worked very closely with the individual growers in order to monitor the progress of each year's crop and to set picking dates for the harvest. There was strict quality control from the moment the grapes arrived at the *cuverie*. Unripe or rotten grapes are refused and payment for the rest depends not just on sugar content (the normal method), but on a whole range of analytical and tasting criteria, designed to reward real quality.

At first, they paid little attention to the white wines, since most went for distillation into Armagnac, but by 1976 they were facing a crisis, for it seemed that most of the Armagnac grapes would have to be torn up because of declining demand. 'We had to sink or survive,' explains Dubosc.

Willingness to concede that other wine-producing regions of the world have anything to teach them is not a quality that typifies most

French growers. Quite the reverse. It is a measure both of their desperate plight and their uncommon intelligence that the *vignerons* of Plaimont decided to go abroad to learn the modern techniques of white wine vinification. 'Some of the growers went to Geisenheim because our oenologist knew of it,' says Dubosc. After initial suspicion, they realized that German wines were well made (a staggering admission for a Frenchman). But they were horrified at the quality of the grapes. 'They make good wine with bad grapes, but we make bad wine with good grapes!'

So they started accumulating funds, preparing for the investment in modern, temperature-controlled vinification equipment that they knew to be necessary. And they travelled. Every year Georges Lascun, their president, organizes trips to the principal vineyards of France, Italy, Spain and Portugal.

In 1981 they poured their accumulated resources, plus all the low-interest capital they could lay their hands on, into a major investment at St Mont. Ten million francs were spent in installing stainless steel *cuves*, pneumatic presses, centrifuges and a refrigeration plant. And the investment has continued year by year.

Unlike so many co-operatives which have mortgaged their future to acquire the latest high-tech wineries, the men of Plaimont didn't sit back and congratulate themselves on all the gleaming tanks and pipework, while continuing with the same old haphazard ways. They actually know what to do with their expensive equipment.

In the first place they use only the free-run juice from the destalked grapes, discarding the press-wine for distillation into Armagnac. This allows them to make wine which retains all the delicate, aromatic qualities of the grapes. They ferment this juice, clarified by centrifuge, with selected yeasts at a controlled low temperature for about fifteen days. It is then racked off its lees and filtered through Kieselguhr, in order to avoid the malolactic fermentation and preserve the fresh, lively character of the young wine. They ensure that this delicacy is not lost during the course of the year by storing their whites until bottling in large tanks, under inert gas. And they have a fully sterile bottling-line.

All this is overseen by Claude Houbard, an oenologist who has worked with Pierre Dubourdieu, owner of Château Doisy Daene, and one of the most innovative white wine-makers of Bordeaux. It was a trip to California (inconceivable a few years earlier) that stimulated their latest and potentially most successful development.

They saw some of the most advanced wineries in the world, and they discovered Parducci's 'French Colombard'. This immensely gulpable stuff – light, dry but with soft fruit at the finish – was for the men of Plaimont a startling revelation. Back home in Gascony, Colombard was the least valued of their grape varieties, producing the sort of thin, acidic wine which was considered perfect for distillation. Nobody thought of drinking it.

They realized in California that, by fermenting it carefully to preserve a fresh, aromatic quality, and by leaving a little residual sugar in the wine, they could produce Colombard that was immensely saleable; with the natural acidity softened by a touch of sweetness.

Unfortunately, they called this delicious plonk 'Vin de Pays des Côtes de Gascogne', with 'Cépage Colombard' in small print at the bottom of the label. This mouthful of words proved too much. Sales were modest in France, non-existent overseas. But the Plaimont Co-operative allowed me to redesign the label for my shipments to England, giving prominence to Colombard and second place to 'Vin de Pays. . . .' And they adopted the revised version as their standard label in France. The wine is doing rather well.

The Co-operative wins endless medals at the wine fairs, but they are not content to sit in St Mont, waiting for the world to come running to the door. Monsieur Lescun has organized a team of growers who travel all over France, dressed in berets and vignerons' aprons, promoting the theme 'Gascony in a bottle'. The sales office, under Jean-Luc Garnier, has organized enormous public relations gatherings at St Mont, poster campaigns, promotional material for the restaurants and sponsorship of the local rugby league (Dubosc used to be a keen player). It is all very professionally done.

But they remain countrymen who grow cereals, breed cattle, raise ducks and geese as well as prune their vines. This is not an area of monoculture, and both the landscape and the people seem more interesting as a result. The Plaimont Co-operative fits wonderfully well into this locality, expressing all that is best about the sense of place, which is one of the most important elements of all good wine.

I arrived there one Saturday in spring, a bright day with clouds making dappled shadows on the landscape. It was past midday, a time when it is rare to find anyone around during the week, let alone at the weekend. Yet there were Messieurs Lescun, Dubosc and Garnier waiting to greet us. A quick tour of the winery was followed by a drive through wonderful countryside to a neighbouring hamlet.

I travelled with Jean-Luc, bouncing along in his 2CV van, the sides of which proclaim the Co-operative's motto. It was a cheerful way to go to lunch.

The restaurant, Le Relais d' Armagnac, is renowned as a family place that produces vigorous classic food. Sitting there with Irène, our hosts and Richard Tanner, eating a wonderful meal and listening to the chatter (while contemplating the beautiful, sickle face of the girl who served us) was a simple, restful delight.

This is a place to come back to, a region that deserves further exploration. The pursuit of wine is rewarded, once again, by the discovery of a landscape and its people.

V
State of the Future: California

The Cycles of Change

The dawn of California viticulture, according to many enthusiasts, was 1966: the year that Robert Mondavi left his family business to build the first completely new winery in Napa since Prohibition. But this is to ignore a colourful history that stretches back to the early Mission Fathers, and which has startling parallels with more recent times.

The first California wine was produced by Spanish missionaries for sacramental purposes. In 1849, the pace of life dramatically altered. It was Gold Rush, and within three years, San Francisco grew from a sleepy village of 800 souls to a boom-town of 92,000. Two-thirds of this number were thirsty miners and, in 1852, they consumed over 60,000 gallons of local wine. It was poor stuff: the produce of native American vines, grown in the area of Santa Barbara and Los Angeles. But this explosive market growth attracted serious viticulturalists.

The most flamboyant was a Hungarian, Colonel Agoston Haraszthy, who pioneered the wine-growing areas north of the Bay, and the introduction of the noble vine varieties of Europe. When he set up the Buena Vista winery at Sonoma in 1857, it was as great a turning-point for the nineteenth-century wine industry as was Mondavi's establishment in recent times. Within a couple of decades, wine was big business. The newly formed University of California provided technical guidance; immigration from the phylloxera-devastated vineyards of Europe provided the labour; the booming economy of the American West provided both the customers and the capital. By the turn of the century, there were over a hundred wineries in the Napa Valley, and the structure of the industry was established in the image that endures today.

America then was a nation of wine-drinkers. It was Prohibition (1919–33) that introduced the delights of bootlegged beer, hard liquor and organized crime. For the wine-growers, it was a disaster. A few survived, licensed to make wine for sacramental and medicinal purposes. As in Chicago, it was the Italians who prospered during this era, using their traditional contempt for unenforceable law to establish for themselves a corner of the market. Old man Parducci kept on producing 'altar wine' discreetly out of the way in Sonoma County. The canny Louis Martini stockpiled his best wines for twenty years, making a fortune when he finally released them in 1940.

After the war, another wave of immigrants from Europe brought viticultural experience and, once more, this was enhanced by the research undertaken at the University of California. The Golden State experienced another Gold Rush as space technology, the entertainment industry and the mighty chip provided the wine-makers, amongst others, with a prosperous clientele, and a new wave of wealthy investors. A century after the Napa Valley had first invited comparison with the classic vineyards of Europe, its wines once again demanded, and deserved, international recognition.

'If you want to be a millionaire in the wine business, you must first be a multi-millionaire in some other business.'

Bernie Turgeon

Money has always been important. It was a fortune based on whaling that enabled Alfred Tubbs to import the French stone with which he built the castellated gloom of Château Montelena in the Napa Valley in 1882. The profits of banking financed the Goodman Brothers when they continued a vernacular tradition by raising the great barn of Eschol (now Trefethen) in 1886. In our times, it cost Joseph Phelps $7 million to build and equip his barn, the finest wooden structure in Napa, and when Tom Jordan dreamed of building a French château in the Alexander Valley it was a $20-million dream. Fortunately, he was in the oil business.

In the late 1970s wine sales surged ahead at an enormous rate, and there were any number of wealthy investors prepared to sink their fortunes into flamboyant buildings, stainless steel pipework and fermentation tanks, costly cooling systems, complex bits of high-tech equipment and rows of the traditional oak casks, shipped at enormous expense from France. Today, many of them have been forced to sell at a loss as the market has turned against them.

They should have climbed up the road to old Mrs MacRae, on Stony Hill, to learn how little of this investment was essential. There the hand-picked grapes arrive by jeep at a winery building that is a modest structure of thick stone walls and a well-insulated roof. The crusher and the press are small, and there are a few stainless steel fermentation tanks, but much of the fermentation takes place in well-used oak casks of varying sizes and indeterminate age. The maturation casks, too, are mostly second-hand, and the whole establishment has a pleasantly unassuming air. From these simple surroundings comes one of the very best California Chardonnays.

It was the price of Chardonnay, climbing ever higher, that tempted so many saps into the business. By the 1981 vintage, the top growers were getting over $2,000 per ton and the wineries thought they were giving the stuff away if they charged less than twelve to fifteen dollars per bottle. You can halve those prices today.

> *'The strength of the dollar is killing us.'*
>
> **Michael Mondavi**

When I first started importing California wines in 1981 the exchange rate gave us over $2.40 to the pound. Today the rate of exchange has fallen dramatically. This has not only made California wines twice as expensive on the export markets, but also, much more to the point, it has halved the cost of French and Italian wines to the American importers. Competition from low-cost imports hits the domestic producers extremely hard. They had to lower their prices a very long way in order to survive.

It may have hurt the great names like Mondavi, but they have the resources to come through and to prosper. After cutting the price of their Fumé Blanc from nine dollars to seven, they have had to put it on allocation, so buoyant is the demand. The small wineries, however, have experienced really lean times and many have changed hands, at 'distressed prices'. It is startlingly similar to the pattern of a century ago, when a swift rise in prices as California wines obtained increasing international esteem was followed by an even more rapid collapse.

The loss of confidence that has resulted from these financial problems has been accompanied, perhaps coincidentally, by some diminishing of technological optimism. There is a growing interest in the traditional ways of Europe, an increasing sense that not all the answers can be found in the laboratory.

> *'We're in the forefront from the oenological and technological standpoint but we have a tremendous amount to learn about the soil and viticulture.'*

> **Michael Mondavi**

The admission is one that many California wine-makers still find hard to accept. Joe Heitz told me firmly: 'It's a lot of hokum that vines have to be old to grow good wine. It's a lot of hokum that vines have to grow on a hillside to grow good wine.' This opinion is shared by Bill Jekel and others who believe that adequate drainage, together with sunshine and a controlled amount of water, constitute most of what is needed to produce ripe, healthy and good quality grapes. They think that most Frenchmen (together with Dick Graff at Chalone and Paul Draper at Ridge) are kidding themselves when they emphasize the importance of location and 'stress'.

It is significant that Michael Mondavi, president of the most technically advanced winery in California (perhaps in the world), should have revised his beliefs on the subject. 'Ten to fifteen years ago I agreed with Joe Heitz, but from our own research I've had to re-evaluate that opinion. To date we don't have complete understanding. I can show you samples from different parcels of wine, with the only variable being the soil. There are huge differences. Let me give you an example. Our Cabernet Reserve comes from Block P, contiguous to Joe Heitz's "Martha's Vineyard". Between Martha's Vineyard and ours is a row of eucalyptus trees, very old, We've made wines out of the first four rows next to the eucalyptus trees, and the next four rows, and the next four rows. We have taken soil samples. There is a distinct eucalyptus flavour in the soil close to the trees, because for a hundred years the leaves and nuts have fallen there. And you can taste that in the wine.'

Sometimes you feel that all Californians are descended from Doubting Thomas – they have to prove to themselves what to others seems self-evident.

'I pay attention to the art of winemaking rather than the science.'

Mike Grgich

As with viticulture, so with vinification. The pendulum is swinging from the technological brilliance, the antiseptic environment and the fascination with control systems of the California that produced NASA and Silicon Valley, to the West Coast enthusiasm for things organic; for wholefood and natural processes; for traditional ways. Both streams of thought are reconciled in wineries like Ridge or Phelps; structures of recycled timber filled with gleaming devices of stainless steel.

There is still a good deal of experimentation – witness Dr Kunkee's experiments with the genetic engineering of yeast cultures, or Ridge's investigation of components of colour and taste by means of nuclear magnetic resonance. But, equally, there is a revival of all manner of traditional ways, whether of barrel-fermented Chardonnay or three-week skin contact for Cabernet. Michael Mondavi even tells the story of a couple of old vintners who were so worried about the effect of replacing all the copper and brass pipes with stainless steel, that they hammered huge copper nails into the backs of the gates in their stainless steel tanks. Recent investigation into the effect of trace elements suggests that they were right! As Michael says, 'The worm always turns.'

One could repeat the story, in different guises, for almost every aspect of viticulture and vinification. Overall it is clear that while the research goes on unabated, this is also a time of consolidation. 'We have been advancing so fast that we haven't been able to notice the fine tuning. And now that we are doing the fine tuning we begin to see the enormous difference that soil makes.' Michael Mondavi's remark can be repeated in relation to all manner of traditional assumptions that were thrown overboard in the headlong rush of the 1970s. We can expect California wines in the future to be more consistent; to establish their identity in the context not only of the technical brilliance of the wine-making systems, but with reference to the traditions that are as much part of California's own past as of the European experience.

It is for this reason that I have chosen to concentrate, in this chapter, on two producers who express that sense of continuity.

Ridge: Paul Draper

California wine-makers are great talkers. No one matches Robert Mondavi in full flow for sheer unstoppable enthusiasm, though some come close. Paul Draper, wine-maker and partner at Ridge Vineyards, is amongst the most thoughtful and interesting.

He is of that original laid-back California generation which emerged from the days of the first hippies with a desire to employ advanced technology in small-scale, 'organic' enterprises. Draper was originally from Chicago but he went to California, graduated from Stanford with a degree in philosophy, and struck up a friendship with Fritz Maytag, heir to a washing-machine fortune. 'For about eighty years they made the single finest washing machine in America. They didn't believe in planned obsolescence.'

Maytag went on to start the Anchor Steam Brewery in San Francisco, making the best beer on the West Coast, and, together with Paul Draper, he dreamed up a scheme for an agricultural development foundation to work in Central and South America. It was a tiny three-man organization that set up a couple of small projects in Costa Rica and Peru, and a bigger one in Chile, concentrating on soya beans as a high-protein food supplement.

'We decided we could better spend our money if we could set up a business in Chile that would pay my salary, so we decided to work on improving the standards of Chilean wine for export. We hoped to work with the traditional producers, but soon found that we were really going to have to do the whole thing ourselves. So we leased a winery, and some vineyards in the coastal range of Chile, and began to produce Cabernet Sauvignon,' says Draper.

In this roundabout way Draper discovered his vocation. It soon became clear that the Chilean operation was untenable, for economic and political reasons, and in 1969 Paul returned to California.

Maytag owned the York Creek vineyard which supplied grapes to the already renowned Ridge winery, established in 1959 by a gang of bearded academics as a weekend hobby. The moving force was Dave Bennion, then with the Stanford Research Institute, and it was he who acted as wine-maker for the first ten years. Draper appeared on the scene at the right moment to take over. He joined as wine-maker and then became equal partner with the original investors.

The place is spectacularly located, up a dirt track high in the Santa Cruz mountains south of San Francisco, with views of the Pacific and the Bay far below. There is an 'ethnic' wooden shed, built by Bennion and his friends, and further up the ridge is the old Monte Bello winery, which started in the nineteenth century and now houses the ever-changing assortment of wine-making equipment with which Paul Draper produces some of the most distinctive red wines of California.

'We're aiming for wines that, when mature, are as complex and as exciting as possible, wines of great interest. To do that, we feel that we have to start with a full deck – we have to start with young wine that has as much as the grapes can offer. It takes low yields from poor soil to produce this intensity.'

Draper is a great believer in 'stressed' vines of great age, grown in difficult conditions. The classic Monte Bello Cabernet from vineyards near the winery epitomizes what he is looking for. The oldest vines were planted in the last century, over 2,000 feet above sea level, and it snows up there every winter. There is almost no topsoil, and the yield is about two and a half tons per acre, roughly the same as a top Bordeaux vineyard and less than a third the quantity that is produced on the valley floor in Napa. Such vineyards are hard to find. Maytag's York Creek vineyard has sixty-year-old vines of Petite Sirah and also produces fine Cabernet, but it was their search for old vineyards on the hillsides that led the partners of Ridge to rediscover the classic virtues of Zinfandel. Again and again they came across patches of this vine, planted by Italian settlers before Prohibition. They began to realize that it was capable of producing something much finer than the 'jug' wines of the big-production wineries. 'It has the potential of being one of the great red wines of the world,' claims Draper.

If this emphasis on low yield and poor soil sounds traditionally European (quite unlike the 'We control the environment' approach of Bill Jekel), so do many of Draper's ideas on vinification.

'California traditionally used many of the same techniques as Bordeaux. Then came Prohibition. When wine production revived in the fifties and sixties it was a whole new industry and a lot of research came to dominate this second phase. A lot of traditional methods were lost. We made a very serious turn in that road. I have looked back at the traditional California approach, and we have gone back to that in hand-making our wines.'

'Hand-making' means using the natural yeast strains, rather than cultivated commercial varieties. 'Two or three strains usually develop. . . . Over-clean fermentation produces wines that lack complexity. It does not give the aldehydes and volatile acidity which are necessary.' The 'cap' of skins and pulp is held below the surface of the fermenting must by a special stainless steel grid, designed by Draper, and they practise long 'skin-contact', with fermentations lasting anything up to twenty days.

'We are *not* aiming for the biggest wine possible, but we *do* want richness of character and depth of colour, some of which will be lost in the barrel-ageing as the wines gain complexity. I certainly do want to make wines that have elegance, but not in a light style.'

Draper claims that Mondavi is now going for much longer fermentation than before: 'But then through extensive fining and handling, they try to pare the wines down to mature earlier.'

None of that at Ridge, where handling is kept to a minimum, and filtration is virtually unknown. They rack the wines every three to four months in the first year; every four to six months in the second.

This sounds very much like the practice of the best *vignerons* in Europe, but there is a difference. For Draper uses modern techniques in the spirit that imbued the *Last Whole Earth Catalog* (subtitled 'Access to Tools'); a quintessentially Californian publication that combined the ideal of self-sufficiency with twentieth-century technology.

'We already know enough that we haven't fully absorbed as an industry. People are settling down now and saying that we have some basic tools to use and to perfect. But we have continued to do research, to understand what the traditional techniques do and why. We use high-pressure liquid chromotography and nuclear magnetic resonance – we're looking at flavenoids and colour and tannins. Very little work has been done on this over here, in fact the best work on tannins has been done in England, initially with tea!

'We think that this is a tool that can tell us better when to pick a particular variety or even a particular vineyard, how long to ferment on the skins and how often we want to rack. . . . But that's broad research – it's not something that's going to change the way we do things today.'

It is a relaxed attitude that also typifies Paul's stance on that other great source of controversy, the question of maturation in oak. At Ridge most of the barrels are American oak, something that many small wineries would sneer at, following Mondavi's exhaustive research on this complex subject. The general feeling is that French oak casks, made by French coopers, are worth their inordinate cost (two or three times the price of an American oak barrel). Draper acknowledges that there are significant differences between French and American oak, but considers that the major disadvantage of the native product is not the wood but the way that it is seasoned.

'Unless you know what you're doing with American oak the cooper simply kiln-dries the stave. I seek out special lots of air-dried wood that's been held for at least three years. When you air-dry the stave after cutting, it sits out in the open, exposed to wind and rain and sunshine, and that leaches the harsh elements out of the wood. We have nothing but air-dried oak in the winery.'

Whatever the arguments about methods, the results, indisputably, are some of the grandest red wines of California, having that very intensity and complexity which Paul Draper aims for. Elegance becomes apparent as the wines mature, especially in the Monte Bello Cabernet which is often regarded as California's answer to Château Latour. It is a comparison that pleases Draper.

Paul is secure in the knowledge that at Ridge they can still sell their wines at prices that justify the low yields, the concentrated care and attention to detail, the ongoing research. 'As long as this unacceptably strong dollar continues, life in the California wine industry is going to be very tough. People who make real quality and have an established name will survive. Others won't. The increase in wine consumption in the States – so tremendous through the late seventies – is slowing down.'

But he is in a mood of great optimism as they bring in the last of the 1984 vintage. 'It looks exceedingly good. We've never been able to pick the vineyards in such perfect order.' And the philosophy graduate of Stanford is not above his own bit of home-spun:

'I guess that the excitement that viticulture has to offer is the striving for excellence. There's no great satisfaction in a simple product; the satisfaction is in the attempt to produce the greatest that you can. . . . It is a way of life. It connects you with the soil, and that means with something about the way we relate to the earth. It's not so much about wine as about people.'

John Parducci

The Napa Valley is what everyone thinks of when California wine is mentioned, and it is indeed the centre of renown, crammed with more expensive wineries per acre than anywhere else in the state. It can give you vinous indigestion. But at the northern end of the Valley you reach the town of Calistoga, and immediately forget about wine. The place was founded on mud baths and hot springs and they still sell Calistoga water, bottled and slightly sulphurous. There is a geyser nearby, dubbed Old Faithful, which erupts periodically in a great jet of steam and hot water, high into the air. They say it comes from the bowels of the earth. It certainly smells like it.

North again, and you pass through the Russian River district in Sonoma County. The wineries and vineyards thin out and, as you travel through this undulating countryside of red earth and clapboard farms, the pace of life appears to slow. You are in Mendocino County, a rural place centred on a sleepy town, Ukiah.

Visiting Parducci feels somehow like coming home. The bottling and storage cellars are in a low building with a cheerful gift shop and tasting room tacked onto the front. Brick arches and trellises abound. As you walk back up behind to a fold in the hills, to the older winery building itself, you pass a cluster of whitewashed cottages inhabited by various members of the Parducci family. There are a few sleeping cats, and lots of geraniums and apples stored in the shed for winter; the impression is of red-checked table cloths, of pasta, of family life. It is a far cry from 'those monasteries that they're building', as John Parducci calls the numerous, expensive wineries that have sprung up to the south in recent years.

The family is from Lucca in Tuscany, and they all speak Italian, though John's father and mother were both born in California. Adolph Parducci did, however, spend ten formative years of his life in Italy, between the ages of six and sixteen, and he learnt about wine in the family vineyards. Back in California he established a small winery at Cloverdale in Sonoma County. He sold bulk wine to individuals (there were a lot of Italian settlers in those parts), and switched to producing altar wine during Prohibition. All those devout Catholic neighbours of Parducci got through plenty of altar wine, since Sonoma County was well off the beat of most enforcement officers.

With the end of Prohibition in sight, Adolph and his four sons started planting vineyards in Mendocino and, in 1932, they built themselves a new winery on Pine Mountain Ranch, just north of Ukiah.

The company achieved a good reputation for its generic wines (Burgundy, Chablis and the like), but most of the business was still in bulk wines. John Parducci and his brother George realized that there was a developing market for California wine of real quality, and in 1961 they bought out their father and brothers. They built up the size of the vineyards (450 acres today), and were the first people in Mendocino to plant the classic grape varieties on any serious scale. In 1968 the first of these varietals began to appear under their own label.

'As the wineries started to make wines that the consumers liked, there was a big increase in demand. People went on diets, eating fish and fowl and went off the booze kick.' No more Dry Martini lunches but instead a surge in the sales of wine.

By 1972 Parducci was beginning to sell outside California, and they now cover practically every state in the USA. The expansion required investment in new bottling facilities and storage, further vineyard plantings and re-equipment generally. So the brothers sold 80 per cent of their business to raise the necessary finance. Their new partners were 1,800 schoolteachers.

'Teachers didn't have tax shelters or social security, so they formed their own investment company to give themselves some insurance.' The Teachers' Management Investment Company of Newport Beach, California, had to make several approaches to the Parducci brothers before they let them have a share of the business, but they have proved the ideal silent partners. 'They have never bothered us but leave us to get on with running the business. And all those teachers make tremendous marketing tools and great customers.'

John Parducci still dominates the company and has shaped it in his image. He has two sons in the business who help with the winemaking, and a brother, George (modestly described as 'bookkeeper'), who looks after the financial and administrative side. But it is John whose vigorous, honest personality shines through everything they do. Now in his mid-sixties but showing no signs of age, his enthusiasm and his down-to-earth countryman's modesty are irresistible. There is, above all, a sense of quality. 'There is a lot of family feeling, lots of pride. We don't compromise.'

The sense of pride is reflected in the statement that 'Mendocino County wines win more prizes per acre than anywhere else in California', while his modesty prevents him saying that Parducci gets the lion's share of those awards.

The grapes come mostly from their own vineyards, none of which is irrigated. When they buy grapes, John Parducci is happy to pay a premium for quality. 'To produce great wines, the vines have to suffer a little. We buy grapes only from hillside vineyards or those located on what we call "number one bench land". We never buy grapes grown on bottom land, where the soil is rich and deep. Those areas produce a lot of tonnage, but the quality just isn't there.'

Colombard is grown at Home Ranch, beside the winery, and is fermented 'off-dry' to combine crisp acidity with softness at the finish. Parducci was the first to make it this way and has been much imitated (the producers of Plaimont in Gascony being the latest to take up the challenge). 'I've always felt the variety was underclassed,' says John, who is keen to emphasize that 'the sophisticated view can't keep all of us in business. Not everyone can drink Chardonnay or Cabernet.' He is even experimenting with the despised hybrid strains, just in case they prove better than everyone says.

Nonetheless, he does produce all the classic varieties as well. Chardonnay, Sauvignon and Riesling are from the Largo Vineyard, ten miles south of the winery, where the gentle, chalky slopes are cooled by temperate breezes from the nearby Pacific. The Chardonnay is particularly good (I am sipping a glass as I write); clean but full of the character of its variety; medium-weight, elegant and long. It is in no way overstated, having neither the blowsy, oaky fatness of some examples from Napa, nor the grapefruit character of Monterey. Cabernet (excellent), Pinot Noir (less successful) and Gamay Beaujolais (a mistake) are grown on the gravelly soil of the Talmage Vineyard, five miles south-east of the winery in the Ukiah Valley. The Cabernet is supple, well balanced, ready to drink while still young. 'Our customers don't want to wait fifteen years for the wine to soften.'

John is clear about what he is trying to achieve. 'I believe wines should be as natural as they can be, and sold at a reasonable price.'

Nowadays everyone is trying to make lighter wines, and they have been forced by economic circumstances to ask less for them. A few years ago, however, the fashion was all for big, oaky Chardonnays and Cabernets, and it seemed that the wineries could get almost any price if the quantity available was small enough. The Parducci cellars were an oasis of common sense, producing good quantities of their elegant varietals at consistently modest prices. The result was that they won plenty of medals and the loyalty of their customers, but have often been ignored by the critics, who felt cheated if they paid less than fifteen dollars a bottle.

They might still have felt cheated had they visited the winery, for while it is spotlessly clean and well-ordered, there is little sign of the high-tech gadgetry that most California wine-makers consider essential. The fact that the winery is built into the side of a hill allows Parducci to use gravity rather than pumps to a great extent, following John's belief that wine should be touched by as few production processes as possible. Vinification is in stainless steel at a controlled temperature, but that is about the limit of technology. 'Pure' and 'natural' are words that recur again and again – so there is frequent racking but no filtration. Nor did I see a centrifuge. They do have a laboratory, tucked away in a superior shed.

John Parducci is not an enthusiast for oak, and says so frequently. 'Making wine with finesse is ten times harder than making big oaky wine. . . . A quality red wine can become better with some oak-ageing. But it should be the wine you taste, not the wood.'

So oak is used sparingly for the Cellar Master's Selection (small lots of the finest wines), and not at all for the basic varietal range. The whites are held in stainless steel until bottling, and the reds are stored in large redwood tanks, well-seasoned and quite neutral in terms of flavour. Two of these tanks are made from virgin redwood, 'wood that was here before Columbus'.

There is a feeling of simplicity; a sense that Parducci fits more naturally into the traditions of Europe than the headlong technological innovation of California. But, despite the awareness of his Italian roots, John Parducci is emphatically a Californian, and has no nostalgia for the land of his ancestors. 'Their wine-making is so primitive. . . .'

Not quite fair, perhaps, but true enough of a good many growers. It is certainly a sentiment which reflects the mind of a man whose strongly held views are based on continuous experimentation.

While he talks about the natural ways and plays down technique, John Parducci is always trying to do better, to improve his very considerable skills. He is working within a much more sophisticated, open-minded environment than most of his European counterparts.

The latest challenge is to revive the Konocti winery in Lake County, a growers' co-operative that was both mismanaged and under-financed before John and his brother George took a controlling interest. They are concentrating on white wines. 'Eighty million people in the States are not drinking wine at present. When they do start it will be white wine that they try.'

Konocti is now producing a fair amount of Fumé Blanc (Sauvignon), but the big problem was what to do with their acres of Cabernet. John's very Californian answer was simple – make white Cabernet by pressing the grapes quickly and ferment the juice before it has time to pick up colour from the skins. The result, apparently, has a good deal of Cabernet aroma and character, but is fresh, clean and eminently saleable.

Such a solution would probably have been illegal if tried in Europe, such are the restrictions of the *appellation contrôlée* system. Even in California, it seems, there is increasing bureaucratic intervention by people who know nothing about wine. 'It's kinda hard to live with some of the things that go on round here now.'

The tone of voice had something in it of 'Once upon a time in the West'. And you do still feel that pioneering family spirit at Parducci. John took us to lunch in town at a place that was undoubtedly a modern recreation of the Western saloon, but which somehow had the true flavour of the original, full of characters who were typecast for their roles. We ate surprisingly well, and then returned to the winery to make our farewells. John darted across to the apple store and came back with his hands full of fruit which he presented to Irène.

We had visited a very slick winery in the morning before driving up to Mendocino and had grown tired of the marketing jargon and the glossy hand-outs. Parducci's apples tasted *good*.

VI

The Grand Merchants of Bordeaux

The Quai des Chartrons

'No, Agnes, a Bordeaux is not a house of ill-repute.'

George Bain: *Champagne for Breakfast*

The place signifies the people, the Chartronnais: a group of rich bourgeoisie, business rivals but closely related by blood and marriage; a clan that built the prosperity of the Bordeaux wine trade but, in so doing, acquired a reputation for arrogance and ruthlessness through their exploitation of the growers. The clan is now decimated and broken – the result of misfortune and greed. The Quai des Chartrons itself may still house the offices of the famous companies that have dominated Bordeaux for generations, but many of them are now trading shells, owned by multi-national groups. Those few of the clan who have survived have done so through agile adaptation to straitened circumstances. It is increasingly the producers, not the *négociants*, who call the tune.

The fine eighteenth-century buildings, narrow and tall and secretive, were the urban equivalent of the village houses of Burgundy, concealing all behind their deceptive façades. Who would guess that the heavy double doors, with their elaborate brass knockers, were made wide enough to allow wooden hogsheads of wine to be rolled in off the street, or that the cellars stretch a thousand feet back from the road? These days you rarely see hogsheads on the Quai des Chartrons, though road tankers still park on the pavements and pump wine in and out of the cellars through hoses that loop and curl to the peril of passers-by. Even this is becoming a less common sight, and for many visitors the most obvious signs of commerce have nothing to do with wine, but are centred on a number of sleazy cafés whose girls welcome seamen from the docks across the road.

It was these docks on the river Garonne that provided the original reason for the merchants to cluster here. Many of them were foreigners and thus forbidden to settle within the old city walls. Expatriate Anglo-Irish men like Barton and Johnston, Lawton and Lynch dominated a group that included Scandinavians, Dutchmen, Germans and Scots, as well as a few French. They began to arrive in the eighteenth century and grew enormously rich, at the expense of the native proprietors who had no direct access to the export markets, and who were thus at the mercy of the newcomers. For it was the English who consumed almost the entire production of the top properties, leaving the rest of the world with the gleanings, and the French were effectively barred from trading with England. They did not, in any case, understand the intricacies of blending wines for the English taste – how to turn fine Bordeaux into the port-sodden squire's idea of claret. Lafite was dosed with Hermitage; lesser wines with strong Spanish red.

Such culinary expertise has been prized until recent times. Together with a near-monopoly of the export markets, it made the *négociants* rich. Barton & Guestier, Nathaniel Johnston, Sichel, de Luze, Ginestet, Eschenauer, Mahler Besse & Cruse; these are only a few of the names that were to be found on the brass plates of the Quai des Chartrons and the nearby streets. They all became château-owners and many of them built fine houses. It was their money that was responsible for much of the elegance of present-day Bordeaux.

But things have changed. Few of the companies mentioned above have survived in anything like their original form, and dozens of others have gone to the wall. Many factors brought about this irreversible decline in the power of the traditional *négociants*, but there is no doubt in anyone's mind about the circumstances that precipitated the final catastrophe. It was the combination of a hugely overpriced vintage in 1972 with the doubling of oil prices by the Arab States in 1973–4. The first was a local disaster – comparable to other crises in the previous couple of hundred years – but its effects were enormously magnified by the second, the international shock.

Prices had risen rapidly prior to the crash as the growers gained the upper hand. When disaster struck, it was the *négociants* who suffered, for they found themselves locked into expensive exclusivity arrangements which forced them to continue to buy, and which lumbered them with overpriced and unsaleable stock. Their own greed and their madly optimistic belief in the endless continuation of the rising market had led them into the trap which closed with considerable force on the heads of numerous old Chartrons families. There were mountainous debts from which they were only rescued by the injection of outside capital (from British, American and French multi-national groups), and inevitably the old guard found themselves summarily evicted, not only from their companies but also, quite often, from their estates.

The pace of evolutionary change is likely to accelerate. Those who survive will have to be flexible, able to adapt in the future as they have in the past few years to enormous upheavals in their commercial life. The problems are already apparent.

In the first place, the *négociant*'s activity as *éléveur*, as a buyer of wine in bulk which he matures in cask before bottling, has greatly declined. The fact that the *négociant* can often do a better job than the small château is irrelevant to the consumer, who considers, with some justification, that the long history and numerous scandals of blending are sufficient to taint with suspicion any single-vineyard wine that does not bear the 'guarantee' of estate-bottling.

Moreover the *négociant* finds it difficult to finance stock, while the grower has tax and other financial advantages that enable him to hold his own wine and to modernize his bottling equipment. There has been an enormous growth in direct sales from château to consumer and to overseas merchant, so the merchant now has to offer an outstanding selection and much-improved service to justify his position. He also has to operate on lower margins if he is to remain competitive.

There still remains the merchant's expertise in producing consistent blends of generic wines like Bordeaux Rouge or St Emilion but here, too, there are difficulties. At the basic 'own-label' end of the market they are selling largely to the supermarkets, and they compete in a cut-price world. Many companies have seen the establishment of their own brand (another Mouton Cadet) as the way out of this dilemma, but no one has yet succeeded on any substantial scale. The marketing men, from the brewers, the distillers, the champagne producers and the perfume companies (who own many of the famous *négociants*), continue to waste huge resources in the pursuit of their elusive goal.

So what is keeping the *négociants* afloat? For some it is sheer quality (this is rare); for others it is the ownership of properties. But a good many still rely on the pickings of the *cru classé*, or top châteaux, market, the old standby of the traditional firms. In recent times this has been a highly profitable business for the market has been buoyant, aided by a series of good vintages and a strong dollar. Sooner or later there must be a slump, accompanied by a further shaking-out of the trade. The lightweight broker/*négociant* hybrids will replace more of the old firms, and the château-owners will increasingly have the sense to approach their markets direct. The decision of Eric de Rothschild of Lafite to bypass the *négociants* in his dealings with some of his overseas customers is a portent of things to come.

But there are companies which have been able to redefine the traditional role of the *négociant*, and which will undoubtedly continue to flourish. This chapter concerns three of them.

J.-P. Moueix, Libourne

His father was from Corrèze in the Massif Central. *'Mou'* means a soft, wet and muddy land, a place of marsh and lake, and *'eix'* comes from the Latin *'ex'*, an indication of origin. So Moueix means 'from the mud'. But today Jean-Pierre Moueix is referred to as Monseigneur, Le Roi Soleil, the Prince. He dominates St Emilion and Pomerol with uncontested authority.

Corrèze was a region of large families and little money. Unlike most of France (where inheritance is divided equally amongst siblings), they practised the *droit d'aînesse*, the right of the firstborn. There wasn't enough to go round, so the younger sons used to leave home for Paris, to work in the cafés (many of which they now own), or head for Bordeaux, to make a living in wine.

They were considered uncouth by the closed society of the Quai des Chartrons, and their talent for hard work was insufficient to prise them an opening in Bordeaux itself. Outcasts from the city (as the proud Chartronnais had originally been), they settled 'on the other side of the river' from the classic vineyards of the Médoc, Graves and Sauternes in the region of St Emilion. They made the small town of Libourne their centre of operations.

Several families from Corrèze are now prominent in the St Emilion trade, and one (the Bories), even managed to acquire a string of grand properties in the Médoc. But none of them have emulated the spectacular rise of Jean-Pierre Moueix.

1930 was a desperate time to arrive in Bordeaux. Following the crash of 1929 there was a succession of appalling vintages in the 1930s, and the major export markets stopped buying – Britain because of a slump in the value of the pound, Germany because it was in chaos. Even the top properties made a loss, year after year, and other châteaux were lucky if they could sell their harvest at the price of the meanest *vin ordinaire*.

This was the moment that Jean-Pierre's father appeared 'from the mud' and bought Château Fonroque, a property in St Emilion. He had, at least, little problem in paying for his purchase. The vineyard was almost given away, and payments were staggered over several years. But he couldn't sell his wine. So Jean-Pierre, aged seventeen or eighteen, was sent to the north of France in search of customers.

He proved a wonderful salesman. Within a year or two he was selling the wines of several of his father's neighbours, and slowly he became a wine merchant. He formally set himself up as a *négociant* in 1937, and moved to his present cellars on the Quai du Priourat in 1946. This is a grand establishment and the initials 'JPM' are found everywhere, evidence of excusable pride in his formidable achievement.

But this was only the start, for Jean-Pierre was saving for his next coup. The vineyard owners were still having a lean time, interspersed with occasional years of prosperity, and property prices were low. After the dreary vintages of 1950 and 1951 they dipped lower still, especially in the unfashionable areas of St Emilion and Pomerol. In 1952-3 Jean-Pierre Moueix bought four châteaux: Magdelaine in St Emilion; Trotanoy, Lagrange and La Fleur Pétrus in Pomerol. He paid a very reasonable price. And he kept on buying vineyards in the 60s, while reaching agreement with several other proprietors to farm their land, making and selling all the wine. Today Moueix controls the production of eighteen vineyards, ranging from the grandest properties of his region to some recently purchased estates in Fronsac. In addition, he has the right to sell a considerable portion of the crop of Ausone and of Cheval

Blanc, plus numerous similar arrangements with a host of lesser châteaux.

The jewel, of course, is Château Pétrus. Moueix, the *négociant*, acquired the exclusivity for the wines of this property in 1945 when it was hardly known. Only its owner, Madame Loubat, and Jean-Pierre himself really appreciated the extraordinary quality of its wine. They made a formidable team. With none of the flamboyance of Philippe de Rothschild at Mouton, without seeking any formal classification for the wine, or spending a penny to redesign the hideously old-fashioned label, Jean-Pierre quietly made Pétrus the most sought-after wine in the world, consistently more expensive than the first growths of the Médoc.

In 1964 he bought a half-share in the property and, since then, Moueix has lavished on the tiny vineyards of Pétrus the full resources of his empire.

Meanwhile, Moueix had become an art collector. Unobtrusively, but on a staggering scale, Jean-Pierre had been buying paintings since his early twenties. His eclectic but distinctly personal collection now ranges from a superb pre-Columbian mask, to works by Rothko and Francis Bacon. His first Impressionists were acquired in the 1940s, but he has focused most of his attention on twentieth-century masters, with particular emphasis on two quite dissimilar artists: Picasso and Nicolas de Staël.

I once asked his son Christian whether, having swapped a painting for his half-share of Pétrus, Jean-Pierre had ever sold a vineyard to buy a painting. There was a stunned silence. 'Never!' was the emphatic reply.

The love of art and literature, of French culture in all its forms, of language, is a manifestation of Jean-Pierre's most impressive and secret achievement, the making of himself. The first thing that struck me when we met, years ago, was the extraordinary purity and clarity of his use of French. Wonderfully articulated and elegantly phrased sentences succeeded one another, building with instinctive courtesy on my slightest remark. Tall, calm and elegant, despite the drabness of his habitual grey suit, Jean-Pierre radiates the subtle intelligence of a Renaissance diplomat. Where did he learn this remarkable demeanour? 'Our ancestors were peasants,' says Christian, 'but there was a lot of dignity in the family.' There still is, and it is on this base that Jean-Pierre has built, unaided, the structure of his own civilization. Throughout his life, in all its aspects, one has the impression of a ferocious ambition to make good, tamed and directed by a determination to remain true to the country tradition, whereby a word and a handshake are enough to guarantee the most complex of verbal agreements.

This attitude to business was tested to the limit in the crisis of 1973–4. Moueix was faced with a double problem, with commitments to buy from numerous small growers and clamours for help from his customers, saddled with expensive and unsaleable purchases of the 1972 vintage. He honoured both sets of obligations, at enormous cost to his firm. They survived, thanks to their estates and to Jean-Pierre's cautious habit of valuing his enormous stocks at historic cost, rather than at current market levels. But it was a terrible time for a man who had worked so long to build his empire. 'For two or three years he was very pessimistic. It was so hard for him to start rebuilding everything. I have great admiration for what he did.' Christian's words are echoed by anyone who had dealings with Moueix at that time.

The company has revived and now flourishes, but there remains a sense of modest frugality in the comfortable, old-fashioned air of the offices in Libourne. They have remained unchanged for years, even down to the ugly little funnel in the tasting-room, through which the glasses are carefully emptied back into the opened bottles. There are piles of dusty reference samples of past shipments, and, beside them, a small box containing a heap of laboratory analysis forms from Jean-Claude Berrouet, the Moueix oenologist. This is the only tasting-room I know that contains an ashtray, for Jean-Pierre is an inveterate smoker, flourishing one Gauloise after another in his black cigarette holder. He restrains himself while you taste, but lights up immediately afterwards.

Tasting here is never a marathon; no more than fifteen wines, presented at a rate of five or six at a time, each with its distinctive character. They are all from St Emilion and Pomerol and the neighbouring regions – no excursions into the Médoc or Graves, for Moueix knows his speciality and sticks to it. Though we talk briefly about our impressions, there is no attempt to sell. The wines speak for themselves.

And so to lunch. We sit at the table of Monsieur Moueix, glancing alternately at the peaceful view of the river Dordogne and at a still life by Bonnard, sipping sensational wines and being served a series of classic dishes, while the conversation ranges from hot air balloons

('*Montgolfières*' is Madame Moueix's wonderfully old-fashioned term) to anecdotes of Francis Bacon, to English metaphysical poetry: this exceeds even our customers' dreams of everyday life in the wine trade!

Nowadays, though, the lunch is as likely to be at Christian's house, a little further upstream. This is an entertaining place, decorated with great wit by Marie-Laure, who is herself remarkably elegant and very funny. They also buy paintings and sculptures, but their collection is more bewildering than Jean-Pierre's. There is some lovely bronze furniture by Giacometti's brother, very peaceful to look at, and a lot of uncomfortable things, including a squashed automobile in the drawing room.

Christian now shares the day-to-day management of the business with his cousin, Jean-Jacques, but he alone controls the vineyards and the wine-making. He is a graduate of Davis in California; brilliant, thoughtful and innovative.

'We feel the future is more and more in the estates rather than as wine merchants. The merchant's role has been very much weakened in the past fifteen years – we are useful in the poor vintages but, in good years like '82 and '83, the well-known châteaux don't need us – they only need the brokers who take a 5 per cent margin. My father thinks the wine merchant's business will last for another generation, as long as we can keep up our close relationships with the château-owners, many of whom were my friends at school. But an American client came to me recently, and said frankly that he couldn't buy a lot of the wines I showed him because he was being offered them direct from the château.

'We are very strong in generic wines. I think that market will continue because people know that when buying from us we can provide quality. Generic Bordeaux can be beautiful wines as long as people age them properly. I am against the Bordeaux *primeur*.'

Christian is one of the few Bordelais to have a real sense of the international competition, the only one to have told me openly that he feared the entry of Spain into the Common Market 'because many wines of Bordeaux are not of sufficient quality to compete'.

He is equally conscious of the potential of California, despite the problems of exchange rates, and his enthusiasm for the Napa Valley has led him to buy a vineyard there, to make his own wine from scratch.

'I selected the vineyard from the soil. I love the place. I have a very definite idea about soil. It's a feeling. There is no perfect soil to make a wine, but there are good soils for certain conditions. I found three places where I liked the soil. The fact that this one was already planted with old vines (some of them are sixty years old) is a very good sign. Our ancestors picked the best soils.'

He goes there four times a year, for ten days each time. Initially he also sent his staff over to supervise everything, but recently he has trained a team of young Americans in his own methods.

The first (1983) vintage of his wine is scheduled for release in 1986. Christian describes it as 'a sophisticated blend of Cabernet Sauvignon, Merlot and Cabernet Franc, made from a high proportion of old vines'. It is called Dominus, and will undoubtedly sell for a considerable price.

At a more modest level, closer to home, Christian is building up the Moueix domaines in Fronsac.

'I do my best to produce a top wine in California, but I feel I should also do something for my neighbours. I think we can do a lot for the wines of Fronsac – the vineyard is beautiful.'

It is worth remembering that Pomerol was also unknown, fifty years ago.

Pierre Coste, Langon

The first time I visited Pierre Coste it was a wonderful spring day and we walked out into the garden that separates his house from his office. Pierre greeted me in English (not the most notable of his accomplishments), and even attempted a quotation from Wordsworth. I didn't understand a word.

But we sat down and started tasting his wines, spitting into the nearest flowerbed. Monsieur Coste reverted to French for his commentary, and I listened, entranced, to a catalogue of evocative smells and tastes: game, black cherries, fine resin, pepper, woodsmoke, quinine, mint, mulberries, vanilla, hazelnuts, marrons glacés, angelica, figs. Coste has an enormous tasting vocabulary, which he uses with fluency and quite remarkable precision. He is not only one of the best tasters of Bordeaux, but a master of the difficult art of describing sensory impressions.

I realized on my next visit that he didn't have a tasting-room. Tasting-counters are designed for peripatetic sniffers and spitters, but Coste prefers to taste sitting down. So when the weather was cold we had to abandon the garden, and perch on a hard chair in his office, aiming for a small bucket on the floor while trying to balance several glasses, take notes, pass the bottle and keep up with Pierre's flow of French. A messy spitter at the best of times, I was relieved when he announced on my arrival in 1980 that he had designed a tasting-table, which had just been installed, and that I was to inaugurate it. Pierre, his daughter Hélène, a couple of friends and I sat round the table and started spitting out the samples into the shallow trough in the centre. This was neatly constructed so that the wine ricocheted briskly across the table to splash the shirt of whoever was sitting opposite. It became apparent that only by craning the head sideways and spitting horizontally, one at a time, was it possible to avoid disaster. Pierre was unperturbed, much taken with the idea that we should all wear polythene bibs, specially printed with the words *'J'ai craché chez Coste!'*

He is an original, entertaining and eccentric, but he is also a wine-maker of exceptional talent. Coste and a few friends led the wine-making revolution that has resulted in the 'new-style' dry white wines of Bordeaux – fresh, clean, full of fruit but bone dry. Only ten years ago most of the whites of this region were dull and flabby, wavering between semi-dry and medium sweet, fit only to be exported to Germany where they were turned into sparkling sekt.

Coste wrote a pamphlet for the CIVB (Conseil Interprofessionel des Vins de Bordeaux), which was issued to small growers to help them learn better techniques. He had to spell out in detail a series of precautions that now seem elementary, emphasizing the critical importance of picking at the right moment, and of avoiding oxidation between vine and bottle. There are still plenty of growers who have got all the necessary equipment for low-temperature vinification (the vital element in this equation), but who ruin everything by letting truckloads of grapes stew in the sun before getting them to the press house.

As far as Coste is concerned, the process of experimentation and innovation is constant. He quotes Bordeaux's most famous wine professor, Emile Peynaud: 'Tradition is an experiment that has succeeded.' At present, he is trying the effect of up to eight hours maceration of the white grapes prior to pressing and, for his reds, he has devised a new system of *remontage* (the circulation of the fermenting juice over the 'cap' of skins and pulp) in order to get greater extract. He is not aiming for nouveau-style reds but for accessible classics – claret that can be enjoyed while young but which will keep and develop over many years. By harvesting late, to ensure fully mature grapes, and by fermenting at exceptionally high temperature, Coste produces red Bordeaux of remarkable intensity and character, even in the less generous vintages.

He makes wine from his own vineyards and he also vinifies grapes that are grown and harvested with his supervision. It is comparable to the operation of a California winery. And like the top Napa winemakers, Pierre has numerous disciples. 'It is a privilege to work with Monsieur Coste,' exclaims Dmitri Hadjinicolaou, opening another bottle. He had arrived from Greece to study wine in France and, at the end of his studies, he stayed on to work as wine-maker with Pierre. Specializing in the whites, he has struck up a good rapport with his teacher. *'Bon élève,'* says Pierre, sniffing a glass of Dmitri's vinification of a 1983 Bordeaux Blanc.

'Quel maître!' replies Dmitri.

Pierre's most devoted pupil is someone who has been studying his ways since the cradle: his daughter Hélène. They make an entertaining team, turning to each other as they consider each sample, amplifying each other's descriptions in their search for the appropriate word. The entertainment is visual as well as verbal. Pierre is bearded, greying, dressed in a light suit and an open-necked white shirt. The only time I saw him wear a tie was when he came to see me once in England, to be filmed for a television programme. He is getting . . . more substantial. As he says with a rueful smile, 'My envelope is growing.' Hélène, by contrast, is prone to silver bomber jackets and bright pink pants or a mock leopard-skin coat and gold high heels. They are not exactly typical of the Bordeaux trade.

But Coste is a *négociant* as well as a grower and wine-maker. He sells mostly on the French market, through distributors and representatives to the restaurants, and directly to private customers. The representatives work on a mixture of salary and commission, but they are that curious breed, particular to France, with multiple employers from whom they are practically independent. About a third of his trade is export. It has to be said that while he makes and sells the most wonderful wines he is not the best organized of businessmen. This is something that he disputes every time I raise the matter, slightly hurt that I could suggest any lack of efficiency. But his mind is too full of other things to concentrate on the paperwork.

He writes wonderful letters to his customers in France, outlining the character of the new vintage. Each harvest is greeted with an enthusiasm that might seem disproportionate in another man, but which reflects Pierre's remarkable ability to make good wines in the most unpromising circumstances. And his prose is as irresistible as his wine.

Coste is one of only three or four *négociants* who deal seriously on the private customer market. 'In France many private clients drink Bordeaux wine who didn't drink it before. The level of life has changed very much. People who drank *vin de table* now drink *appellation contrôlée*. The consumption of *vin de table* is very much reduced, and the per capita consumption of wine overall has declined from 125 litres in 1958 to about 85 litres now.

'In England it is quite different because the *vin de table* never had the same role as it had in France. In France the consumption of *vin de table* increased with the development of the first industrial society. People tried to find oblivion in wine – they tried to forget their troubles. But now the proletariat is very small, very few in numbers. Now people want to drink Côtes du Rhône or Bordeaux two or three times a week.

'Every day I receive five or six letters, mainly from young people saying "I am not a wine drinker but I want to know more – can you tell me something about Bordeaux wine?" I believe that the wine trade is very different from all other trades because of this rapport with the customers which is quite different to the experience of those who sell shoes, for example. The wine market is a market of pleasure, *de luxe*; it is not a first necessity.'

He is adamant that Bordeaux wines in general are getting better. 'The volume of fine wine has much increased since 1950, the date from which the new oenology greatly improved the quality of Bordeaux. There is ten times more good wine now than there used to be. In Bordeaux it is necessary to change every day.' And he applied this sense of change to the role of the *négociant*, emphasizing that he is not simply buying and selling wine, but advising and assisting the growers as well. 'I work with two or three little proprietors to produce my Bordeaux Supérieur; it's very different from the *grands négoces*. The *négociant* of the future will be a Director of Conscience for the grower, to guide him on the right path.'

The path that we take leads out of the cellars, through the garden and into his house for lunch. The house is filled with a bizarre assortment of works by various artist friends and of objects collected on his travels with his wife. They intersperse journeys to the most out-of-the-way places with pilgrimages to Bayreuth; they are both opera fans, mad Wagncrians.

Lunch is cooked and served by Max, an intriguing figure of uncertain age who looks rather smart from the waist up (in a neat white waiter's coat), but whose rheumatism forces him to shuffle around in a pair of shabby old slippers that Coste refers to as *'pantoufles charentaises'*. His food is superb. We drink a series of samples that we had tasted in the morning, plus a few earlier vintages of Pierre's own wines and a grand bottle of Ducru Beaucaillou or Latour or, occasionally, both. A fine pudding wine from Coste's friend, Pierre Dubourdieu, proprietor of Château Doisy Daëne, is followed by the embarrassing moment when the port appears. The French in general drink tawny port, chilled, as an aperitif, but Pierre persists in thinking that he understands vintage port, that most English of vinous specialities. He ships some dreadful stuff which he flogs to his wretched customers and inflicts on visiting wine merchants. I always try to skip this bit and move on to the Armagnac or cognac, because this is when Pierre gets back on to solid ground and proffers the most wonderful bottles, often of incredible age.

These leisurely lunches are not the only reason to visit Coste, but they are certainly eagerly anticipated. One of my most wretched days in Bordeaux was the time I arrived at Pierre's house and had to watch as the wonderful dishes and the marvellous wines succeeded one another, while I nibbled at a small piece of boiled fish. The day before I had inadvertently drunk a glass of water in St Emilion.

Peter Sichel, Bordeaux

'It sometimes happens that a great vintage is lost in the shadow of its predecessor or, as can be read at French railway crossings, "Attention! Un train peut en cacher un autre".'

Peter Allan Sichel, commenting on the 1970 and 1971 vintages in Bordeaux

There are two Peter Sichels. One is Peter Max, based in New York, who is associated with the international brand of Liebfraumilch that bears the Sichel name. The other is Peter Allan in Bordeaux, well-known in the trade (particularly for his entertaining and erudite vintage reports), but whose company appears under a series of disguises when its wines are shipped abroad to Britain or America. The reasons for this complex state of affairs are buried in a tangled history.

The Bordeaux firm of Sichel seems today a bastion of England, favourite source of supply for innumerable English buyers and centre of Anglo-Saxon gossip. Its origins were quite otherwise. Peter's great-grandfather was Danish, a man called Hermann Nathan who went to Mainz, married a German lady called Sichel, joined the family wine firm and took his wife's name to give confidence to his customers. So the house of Sichel in Bordeaux started in 1883 as the buying office for a German importer. But Hermann junior didn't get on with the German side of the family. He married a Dane and settled in London. In 1920 he and his son Allan finally separated the English importing company from their cousins in Mainz, and retained the organization in Bordeaux as their buying office.

Allan Sichel was a renowned taster and vinous authority, author of a much-respected book on wine, and mentor of a great many students of Bordeaux. But he never lived there, despite having acquired (very inexpensively) a third share in Château Palmer. His son, Peter, was the one to make the permanent move to France. From the age of twenty-one he spent four or five months of every year in Bordeaux, and just before he was thirty he settled there permanently, buying the sadly neglected property of Château d'Angludet.

Angludet had been bought by a Monsieur Rolland, owner of Château Coutet in Barsac, as an estate for his stepson. After the disastrous frosts of 1956, the worst of the afflictions of a cheerless decade in Bordeaux, they virtually abandoned the vines at Angludet and concentrated on breeding a dairy herd. But the stepson showed little interest, and Rolland had to decide between selling Coutet or Angludet. At that time the top sweet wines were selling better than claret from the Médoc, so he relinquished Angludet. Peter bought it for a song.

'There were some extremely old vines (over a hundred years old), and two other plots that had been badly planted ten years previously and were producing nothing of any consequence. I had to replant the whole place.'

For his first vintage in 1961 (one of the greatest years this century), Peter made eleven hogsheads of wine. His average today is 480.

Angludet now is a wonderful cross between England and France. You approach it along a white-fenced drive, past meadows and horses. The house is low, single-storey; a former hunting-box. There are more horses to be seen in the drawing-room, capering around in the lively old murals depicting an eighteenth-century riding school. It is the comfortable, relaxed home of a large and boisterous family – the sort of place where you have supper in the kitchen after a tour of the cellars enjoying a sampling of the young wine. If you feel like walking down the valley to see how the work of clearing the tangled woods has progressed since the last visit there are plenty of wellington boots in the boiler-room.

Peter is habitually dressed in corduroy trousers and a zip-up jersey, whether at home with Diana or sampling wine in the tall, spacious tasting-room on the Quai de Bacalan (an extension of the Quai des Chartrons). His conversation is sufficiently provocative that we tend to disagree a lot, with good humour.

During the 1960s, Peter built up a considerable reputation on account of his selection of unknown *petits châteaux*, and the fact that he was English – a source of great comfort to many a tongue-tied Anglo-Saxon buyer. The business expanded and, eventually, there was a reconciliation with the German cousins, resulting in the amalgamation of their selling efforts on the British and American markets. The Mainz company had made Blue Nun Liebfraumilch into an international best-seller, and it seemed to make good sense to show a united Sichel family rather than one which was competing with itself.

During the boom period before the crash, it seemed to the Bordeaux company that they had found a goldmine. 'We were selling a great deal of wine in America, but we were given no idea that all the wine we were shipping to the States was piling up in people's warehouses. I was told to buy, buy, buy – and I did so with borrowed money.' Peter Sichel built a big new bottling-plant and warehouse at Ludon in the Médoc to cope with the projected expansion from the States, and filled it to the ceiling with wine, including a good deal of the wretched vintage of 1972.

'Came the crash, we were sitting on masses of wine which all of a sudden America didn't want. The value of the wine was falling every day and the cost of financing it was increasing.'

It was the same story for a number of other merchants, and many of them did not survive. Sichel's company very nearly foundered. Peter could have retired to Angludet, but he was grimly determined to pull through.

The warehouse and bottling-plant at Ludon were sold, and the partnership with the German cousins was broken. They retained exclusive right to the Sichel name in England, while Peter's rights in his name in the States were sold to Schieffelin, the Blue Nun agents. They scraped through, contracted back to their original premises on the Quai de Bacalan and reduced the number of employees from fifty-five to thirty-five. And now they are prospering again. Sales are back above the precrash heights, and Sichel's are about to install a fully automated new bottling-line in big new cellars in Bordeaux. The basis of the business is what it always had been: the sale of generic wines to the English-speaking countries.

'When I started, all Bordeaux rouge was being made the same way as Château Latour – and was quite undrinkable. We started to look at ways of making Bordeaux rouge with some fruit and charm.' The answer was the Belair vinification centre that Peter built in 1967 at Verdelais in the Premières Côtes de Bordeaux. The idea is to buy grapes from small growers in the region, which are then vinified under the control of Sichel's own oenologist. They now make about 3,000 hectolitres of wine each year. The red is produced by carbonic maceration, making a soft, appealing wine, full of fruit, which can be used to soften the hard austerity of the more traditional Bordeaux rouge that Sichel's buy in bulk. The white wines vinified at Belair are cold fermented to preserve freshness. Now that everyone else in Bordeaux has woken up to this technique, Peter Sichel is concentrating his efforts on 'off-dry' wines, with a bit of residual sugar, since these are rarely well made by other producers.

The lure of the generic brand is something that has absorbed the efforts of a good many négociants over the years, mostly to no avail, and Peter is realistic about the problems. 'We cannot compete with Seagrams who can throw buckets of money down the drain promoting a brand. . . . But I *do* want to produce a wine under our label, a really first-class generic product. I'm very interested in the difference in image between the California wine-maker and the Bordeaux négociant. I think we can do something about this by concentrating on producing real quality. I am thinking about using new wood for generic Bordeaux, just a short time in cask, in the California manner. It's got to come back to *élevage*, doing something the small grower can't do himself. I shall start experimenting soon – we can begin on a very small scale.'

This ability to test things out, to produce innovative ideas all the time, is going to be vital to the future of the Bordeaux *négociants*. So, it seems to Peter, is a clearer understanding of their *raison d'être*.

'A fundamental thing that people in Bordeaux often get wrong is the idea that *négociants* are there to be the selling agents of the growers. We are there to be the agents of our customers, to understand what they need and to supply it. It's a very personal business – I can personally look after throughout the world from fifty to perhaps a maximum of 100 customers if I want to do it properly. That's why there's room for a lot of us. It's very rare to be strong in all markets; for historic reasons most *négociants* specialize in particular areas and have a great deal of expertise on a limited number of markets.

'You have to cut your cloth accordingly. We are *very* flexible in our approach. If someone is capable of buying large quantities direct from a property we can work on a brokerage basis. We can provide a real service to our customers. For example, we recently went to every single grower in Bourg and Blaye – we know all about them, what they produce, how they sell and so on. If a customer wants something from this area, we now know the best way of finding it.'

One unstated reason for this extensive survey may be that Peter is considering buying more châteaux, at the level of the basic red and white appellations of Bordeaux. 'The fun would be to create something,' a motive close to that which has led Christian Moueix to acquire a couple of properties in Fronsac.

Whatever the opportunities and problems of the future, the Sichel family should be well placed to deal with them, for Peter and Diana have five sons and an afterthought, their six-year-old daughter, Rebecca. Allan, the eldest, is qualifying as a chartered accountant. Charlie has already started in the wine business, and will work in Britain and the States, while his twin Jamie has yet to decide. Ben is destined to the work on the vineyard side after completing his studies in viticulture and oenology at Château La Tour Blanche. David, the youngest, is still at school.

Perhaps the English will finally reconquer Bordeaux.

VII
The Bordeaux Commodity Market

Abe's Sardines

'Abe bought a shipment of sardines that had already been traded many times and each time profitably. Unlike previous buyers, Abe took the trouble of procuring a box of his purchase. The sardines were terrible. He telephoned Joe from whom he had bought them only to be told "But Abe, those sardines are for trading, not eating."'

Peter Sichel related this fable when discussing the spiralling price of first-growth claret in his 1971–2 Bordeaux Vintage Report. It was a time of incipient crisis, a year or so before the big crash.

The cycle goes something like this. A reasonable harvest follows a poor year in Bordeaux. One or two not disinterested parties tell a few gullible journalists that it is the vintage of the decade. Excitement mounts. The next year (which is actually the vintage of the decade) becomes the vintage of the century and demand goes mad. Prices double. There is another decent harvest and the Bordelais think they can pull the same trick. The merchants continue to buy, but their customers are beginning to show some resistance to the new price levels. The next vintage is pretty awful and the price is clearly ridiculous. There is a reaction which turns into a panic slump. Bankruptcies abound and everyone blames the oil crisis.

In actuality there are two sides to the problem. In the first place it is now undeniable that the greatest wines of Bordeaux are traded internationally, as investments. Price fluctuations reflect the speculative volatility of all commodity markets. A great deal is to do with intangible elements of confidence (the excitement of the auction room), as gamblers juggle with the uncertainties of international exchange rates, vintage reputation, the availability of investment capital. As with all such markets there is a tendency towards dangerous instability, wild fluctuations between boom and slump.

Speculation can never be eliminated, though its effects might well be abated by a more open market. But there is a second aspect to the problem, in some ways more serious than the first, which concerns the inflexible structure of the Bordeaux trade itself.

It seems strange that France, renowned for the ideal of liberty, should be so protectionist when it comes to business matters; providing legal, fiscal and institutional frameworks that stifle the evolution of free trade, while ensuring the survival of archaic economic species that have long been extinct elsewhere. The idea of separate functions in trade is very important to the French. They have established endless finely differentiated categories of business activity, each with its legally defined privileges and obligations; each with a particular tax status. And this apparently constricting process is continuing. At a time when even the Americans (the other great talkers about liberty) are finally dismantling the cumbersome regulations that make distributing wine so difficult, the French continue to recategorize the structural hierarchy.

Bordeaux sees the system at its most complete. Most famous châteaux will not sell direct to importers, for example, because if they did so they would become *négociants* and thereby lose the considerable tax advantages of being agricultural producers. So they sell to *négociants*. But even here they don't go direct but through a local broker, a *courtier*.

The *courtier*'s role is to know the producers and to understand the requirements of each *négociant*, to whom he brings samples from those growers whose wines may fit his needs. Having arranged a deal, he is responsible for ensuring that the agreed terms of payment are adhered to, and that the wine which is delivered matches the original sample. For this he takes 2 per cent of the value of the deal.

A good *courtier* can save the *négociant* a great deal of trouble by specializing in a particular region of Bordeaux, and selecting suitable samples from the thousands of properties that are anxious to sell. But his role is absurd when acting as intermediary between the famous château and the respected *négociant*, each of whom have been doing business together for years. When the *négociant* wants a hundred cases of Château X he doesn't telephone the owner, but instead rings a broker, who passes on the message and takes 2 per cent of a valuable deal for doing nothing.

Around the major participants in this endless drama flutter other, catchpenny characters, each with a statutory function to play. There are *courtiers en revente, commissionaires en vin* and others, including that curious breed, the VRP (*voyageur, représentant, placier*), otherwise known as a *représentant multicarte*. All mediate, for profit, between grower and consumer.

This commercial stratification (liberty modified) is matched by social hierarchies of great complexity, which redefine fraternity and equality; survivals of that acute French class-consciousness and snobbery described by Proust. Things have greatly changed, but the relationship between the different sections of the Bordeaux trade continues to mirror these historic divisions. Proprietors of the great châteaux have often been aristocrats, too grand to want to haggle with the *négociants* (rich bourgeoisie) who in turn felt it demeaning to hobnob with the peasant growers, owners of the smaller properties.

For all these reasons, a system has survived that is based on mutual distrust between grower and merchant. Neither party understands or wishes to share the concerns of the other, preferring instead to deal through an intermediary. Naturally it is not in the intermediary's interest to suggest that such suspicions might be abated by dealing direct.

Other reasons that have been advanced are the comfort of dealing with the same faces; the avoidance of payment problems; the expert advice given by the broker to the château on which *négociants* specialize in which areas of the market.

In reality, such a system means that the producers have no direct experience of the market because they never talk to their customers. The much-vaunted expertise of the *négociants* is of limited value because everyone in Bordeaux lives from one 'campaign' to the next, grabbing what they can.

If this château's opening price is seventy francs (per bottle), his neighbour will ask no less, and may well decide to up the rate by a few francs so that the world will know which is the better wine. The *négociant* who has tried to persuade the proprietors to moderate their demands, 'in the interests of market stability', promptly forgets moderation, and offers the wine at 110 francs. After a few days' trading, the price has risen to 130 francs, and it continues to rise until the autumn. So next season's campaign starts with an opening price from the proprietor of 130 francs, and the *négociants* allow their most privileged customers to have a few cases for 220 francs. And so it goes, until the next slump.

The top growers could perfectly well bypass both brokers and *négociants*, as has happened in most other wine-producing areas of France. But the present system offers them an assured market, for minimum effort, and makes a lot of middlemen very rich. Nobody weeps tears for the poor consumer, since the lover of first-growth claret is doomed to unrequited passion unless he, too, has well-lined pockets.

But the rich are not always stupid. There comes a time when the price of pulling a cork seems absurd, even to millionaires. Then the can of sardines is unsaleable, though the label be ever so pretty and the name on the side is Hernandez.

Hernandez: Heart of Gold

Antoine Hernandez sits behind a desk littered with telex messages, an IBM screen at his side to show him the latest stock position. He leans back, and tosses a pile of orders into the air as he answers my question with the smile of a hard-working man who loves his *métier*. 'How is business? Business is fantastic!' Indeed it must be, for Hernandez is the most successful dealer in Bordeaux.

He was born near Barcelona (his mother was a Basque) but his father, an insurance inspector, moved to Bordeaux when Antoine was a child. Hernandez is reticent about his early career, but by 1954 he was established as a *commissionaire en vin*, selling stocks of wine from the châteaux cellars. He combined the advantages of an outsider's viewpoint and a shrewd brain, which he employed to acquire an exceptional understanding of the intricacies of the Bordeaux market. He was a gambler, waiting for his moment.

The opportunity came towards the end of 1969, when Château Léoville Poyferré put on the market the whole of its 1967 vintage – 110 tonneaux; the equivalent of 11,000 cases of claret. None of the traditional Bordeaux *négociants* showed any great interest, but Hernandez tasted a sample, realized that the wine was good and moved fast. He bought the entire parcel for less than seven francs a bottle. It was the sort of coup that few people had even contemplated since Walter Berry's amazing deals in the 1930s. Hernandez had arrived. 'I still keep a hundred cases as a reminder,' he says.

With the profits of that deal he financed a new type of *négociant*'s business, establishing SDVF (Societé de Distribution des Vins Fins) in 1970. The deliberately anonymous name typifies his break with the traditions of the Quai des Chartrons. 'The old *négoces* wanted to make the *marque*, to promote themselves – me, me, me – *stupidité*! All their expensive bottling-lines and large establishments, all of this was ill-placed pride.' Hernandez wanted nothing to do with the marketing of brands or with that other traditional occupation, the *élevage* of wine in cask. He was only interested in château-bottled wines, and was determined to offer his customers a better, more expert service than that provided by his traditional competitors, whose understanding of the export markets had failed to keep pace with the changing realities.

The timing could not have been better. Wine had suddenly become of interest to the press, which declared 1969 to be the vintage of the decade (quite falsely), and then leapt with more justified enthusiasm on the large and excellent harvest of 1970. The stock market was rising, led by feverish speculation in Australian mining shares, and the property boom produced new millionaires every week. There was money to burn, and the investment fever spilled over into the wine business. Prices doubled and redoubled.

Hernandez (aided in those days by Henri Quancard) made a great deal of money and, unlike many others, managed to avoid losing it all in the crash that followed. The slump of 1973–4 was brought about by consumer resistance to the absurdly high prices asked for the dismal 1972 vintage and the retreat became a rout when the first great oil crisis battered the economies of the entire Western world. The *négociants* were left holding huge stocks that were unsaleable at half their book value, and companies which had been famous in Bordeaux for centuries past found themselves bankrupt.

Hernandez had been prudent and was able to contain his losses. With minimal overheads he wriggled through and, at the first sign that prices had stabilized, he started buying again. He purchased the entire 1974 vintage of Château Phelan Segur (an important *cru bourgeois*), and he firmly established his position as a major buyer of several of the top châteaux.

Then came the 1975 vintage. Most of the *négociants* were still dazed, slowly recovering from the slump, but Hernandez went out and tasted at all the leading properties and returned to his office convinced that this was a great year. He contacted his customers telling them that the quality was exceptional, prices were reasonable and that they must buy: 'I started selling good quantities of '75s and made a lot of money for my clients. After a month or two the *négoces* started tasting. "The wines are not bad," they said. "We want to buy a bit." The property-owners replied: "Oh, but we have sold it all to Monsieur Hernandez." Prices started to go up. The train had left the station!'

It was an express train. Prices doubled, and the company that Hernandez had created was at last recognized as a major power in Bordeaux. From this moment, it was clear that the new breed of *négociant* had seized the initiative from the old.

A certain dreary fustiness, that particular smell of dusty, over-stuffed plush furniture, of polish and of typewriter ribbons; the musty scent of chests full of old papers, of tables littered with back-numbers of old magazines: these are the stuff of waiting-rooms to which each profession adds its identifying odour – the whiff of TCP at the doctor's, the aromas of wine on the Quai des Chartrons. From the moment of arrival, SDVF feels different. The offices are light, modern, without unnecessary clutter. There is a quiet hum of activity, and you are never kept waiting more than a few minutes (I have spent long, tedious intervals at some of the traditional *négociants*, while the man I came to see ignored my appointment, and chatted in a loud voice on the telephone in order to impress me with the hectic life of international commerce).

They, themselves, are different, for it would be impossible to suppose for a moment that either Hernandez (father or son) had anything to do with 'old Bordeaux'. They are not above trying to impress (Antoine mentions that he was with Eric de Rothschild yesterday, and Philippe that he was in New York last week with Madame Mentzelopoulos, owner of Château Margaux), but their appearance is so far removed from the guardians of tradition as to make a refreshing break in the pattern of the day. For they remain individual, unlike the Euro-clone marketing men, with their trans-atlantic English, whose obsession with 'brands' is the most tedious aspect of the 'new' Bordeaux.

Antoine has all the charm of a reformed con-man while Philippe, a very snappy dresser, is a fairground roller – the fellow who chats up all the girls as he leaps around the dodgems, collecting the money.

But they offer more than entertainment, for Hernandez is probably the leading exporter of the *grands crus classés*, the best wines of Bordeaux. He is certainly the biggest purchaser of both Lafite and Margaux, and is amongst the top buyers of Mouton and Haut Brion, Pichon Lalande and Ducru Beaucaillou and other renowned properties – '*tous les leaders*', as Philippe says. They are major stockholders, with at least half a million cases at any one time, from all regions of Bordeaux. But their staff remains small (less than fifty over-all), and Hernandez is determined that this is how it will stay. 'We must be very light on our feet, very flexible, not like those huge great mastodons, almost impossible to move. Every ten years in business we must break the mould and rebuild things. The worst thing is a routine – there must be an evolution.'

At the heart of this success is a highly professional service, based on thorough research of production and markets. Hernandez is emphatic that it is this service which justifies his role, and which differentiates the new breed of *négociants* from the old. He despises the '*telexistes*', those intermediaries with an office but no stock, who scavenge what they can by putting out offers over the telex to all and sundry. 'These men come from houses which have folded. Of course everyone has to make a living – but it's not constructive work. They have no commercial shame – they make the same proposition to everyone.' What Hernandez likes is to dream up a deal that is designed specifically for the needs of a particular customer. 'The business of sending out price lists is finished. Everyone is busy. My role is to imagine things which my client may not have thought of, to realize this idea, to bring it into being. That is a huge satisfaction.'

Hernandez, for example, has decided to try to bring some order into the market for older vintages, something that has been highly developed in England through merchants and auctioneers, but which has always been a fragmented, disorganized affair in Bordeaux itself. 'Now we can find old wine for you and give you a reference price within a maximum variation of 5 to 10 per cent of what you will actually pay. We can guarantee the condition of the wine and the level of the bottles, and we can make sure that the bottles are recorked at the château if this is necessary.' The best customers also get an 'after-sales' service, for Philippe travels regularly in the

States, promoting and publicizing the great châteaux, making sure that the wine moves rapidly from importer's warehouse to retailer's store.

Talking to Hernandez one gets the impression of a market that is becoming well-organized through greater professionalism and an awareness of mutual interests. 'There is a relationship, a friendship between our clients and ourselves. Likewise with the proprietors. They have the duty of making and looking after the wine. We sell it. We have a mediating, stabilizing influence, an evident function. It is complementary, logical. *Chacun défend son bifteck!*'

I point out to him that this stabilizing influence, this balance of interests, didn't last very long when the much-vaunted 1982 vintage came onto the market. Bordeaux reverted to its traditional ways: everyone at each other's throat and the devil take the hindmost.

Hernandez responded with the usual arguments – blaming the press for puffing the vintage, and creating a public clamour to which the proprietors responded by holding back up to half their crop from the market, and by abandoning whatever good intentions they may have had about price restraint. 'I know them too well; they won't sell lower than their neighbours for fear their wine will be devalued. And then there was the dollar factor, a very important phenomenon. If the Americans had not come into the market with a strong dollar, prices would not have moved. We are professionals, not speculators, but there are others who created an ambience of tension, of worry.'

The price of the top wines went rocketing up, out of control. 'There is an insolence in the price of the *crus classés* and modesty in the price of the *petits châteaux*. This is a *great* problem. The small property has difficulty in getting a fair return.' But weren't the *négociants*, Hernandez included, much too greedy in their margins? 'I have said and I repeat: 1982 is a great vintage but it has been bought and sold very expensively. There is a legitimate profit, which each member of the family of the wine trade can hope for, but if prices get too high there comes a moment when the consumer finally says "No". He does ultimately control the market.'

What of the future? Will the *négociants* become redundant and the proprietors decide to deal direct with their overseas clients?

'When things go well and vintages sell themselves they start thinking of dealing direct. It's human nature.

'But in this business there is a cycle between fat markets and thin markets. In the thin markets the producers understand the utility of the *négoces*.'

Hernandez works up to his peroration like a priest, or like the cunning politician that he is.

'Let me say one thing, with all sincerity. There is a temptation, human, to deal direct. But there are equal temptations for the Bordelais to work closer together to deal with the export markets, to harmonize the way that business is done. We can, within the family of wine, find a system of relationships that works better. In the domaine of wine there are plenty of stupidities in the way things are done. But there is no other value than the man, than man. And this must be at the heart of what we do. We are all a family on the same boat, and we will all be saved or we will all founder.'

He looks pleased with these fine words but then he shrugs and spreads his hands with a smile. 'But men will be men. When you put your hand on your heart you touch your wallet!'

VIII
More Middlemen

Sticky Fingers

The French word for broker is *'courtier'*, while the translation of the English sense of courtier is *'courtesan'*. One has the impression of treacherous flattery and false protestations of love.

In French language, law and custom there are endless finely defined categories of middlemen, each with special obligations and functions. Broadly speaking they fall into two main species, the *courtiers* and the *représentants*.

The *courtier en vin* (including the sub-species *courtier de campagne, courtier commissionaire, courtier de propriété* and *courtier en revente*) is supposedly responsible to the buyer, who pays him a commission.

The *courtier de campagne*, for example, is a regional broker, taking samples from the growers to the *négoces*. He should check the wine when the purchaser picks it up (many don't), and guarantee all the details of the transaction. For this work he is entitled to a 2 per cent commission from the purchaser, and it is habitual in many areas for the grower to give him an envelope containing cash, a further 3 per cent of the deal. For this composite margin of 5 per cent the broker can do good work or he can, like many, simply merit the dismissive title of sample carrier, *'porteur d'échantillons'*. One member of this coterie has criticized the system with an insider's knowledge: 'Most local brokers survive because neither grower nor *négociant* trusts each other. The growers feel that they would be dishonouring themselves to take a sample to a *négociant* to sell it, and the *négoce* himself doesn't want to go and hobnob with the growers in their cellars. It's the old situation of the bourgeois versus the

grower.' The local *courtier*, of course, plays on such traditional suspicions to his own benefit.

The *représentant*, by contrast, is not really a mediator between
buyer and seller. Whether he styles himself *représentant placier* or
représentant multicartes, his first responsibility is to his employer,
the producer, who rewards him with a mixture of retainer and commission.

In practice both *courtier* and *représentant* tend to ensure that their
impartiality is evident to all concerned by keeping their eyes fixed
firmly on their own interests. As does the *agent commercial*, a loner
who defines his own role.

The major difference between all of these categories, and the
négociant or merchant, is that they deal in other people's stock
while the *négociant* invests his own (or borrowed) capital in purchasing wine for resale. Nonetheless there are plenty of light-weight
négociant businesses, whose operations are much closer in style to
the broker than to the old-fashioned merchants of Bordeaux.

A good many people in the wine trade spend inordinate amounts
of time and effort trying to bypass the middlemen in order to save
themselves a few per cent. Of course there are greedy brokers (between two and five per cent commission is normal – anyone working
on more than seven per cent overall has to argue very hard to justify
his take), and there are plenty of situations where brokers are
unnecessary (I have often found them trying to insinuate their noses
into long-standing arrangements which are no concern of theirs);
but a hard-working middleman is more than worth his price.

He should, if he knows his job, research very carefully what is
available in his region of production and assess the qualitative and
financial factors involved. He should equally well understand the
requirements of his clients, and match their needs to supply. The
broker must ensure that the wine which is supplied is the same as the
sample, and he is responsible for overseeing the buyer's adherence
to the payment terms.

The best export brokers do much more than this. They provide a
managerial and secreterial service for the growers, doing all the
commercial paperwork (the invoicing and legal documentation),
arranging transportation, organizing carrying agents, chasing payment. This professional approach justifies their intervention, since
many small producers are incapable of dealing with the complexities of export in an efficient manner (too much day-to-day

work in vineyard and cellar), and the buyer has rarely got the time to seek out the lesser-known growers without some on-the-spot guidance. But it is time-consuming work, because it depends on continuous personal involvement. There are always new demands being made (every vintage is different), and there is always new business to be sought. The broker must keep in touch with his customers and accompany them when they visit the wine regions, introducing them to the growers, ensuring that they find the wines they need. He will be called on to act as travel agent, bureau de change, interpreter, answering service and post office.

Conversely, he must keep in close touch with the growers. They are proud individuals who nonetheless need tactful advice: on problems of viticulture and vinification; price and payment terms; the state of the export market. He has to look out for the arrival of new growers, and check constantly that those with whom he already deals are able to maintain their standards. He must listen to family problems and give financial advice.

The secret of using a middleman is just that – to use him. Buyers who resent the broker's intermediary role often go straight to the grower when there is a problem, forgetting that this is precisely what the broker is there for. They would save themselves time, money and considerable frustration if they simply asked the broker to do his job. They would also improve the quality of brokerage. Lazy brokers survive as long as their clients make no demands on them.

Middlemen may have sticky fingers but that's because they mix the glue which binds together the whole of the wine trade.

Henri Quancard

I first encountered the name of Henri Quancard on a visit to the Loire and Burgundy with Derek Balls (of Balls Bros, London shippers and wine bar proprietors). Late in the evening and weary from the drive we would arrive at the next hotel on our route to be presented by the receptionist with a 'message from Monsieur Quancard'. Would we visit this or that *négociant* in the region, they were expecting us at such and such an hour. How had this relentless Quancard managed to get hold of our schedule, and what had we done to deserve to be hounded by this avenging angel determined to pack our already crowded days with further tests of stamina? I formed an impression of a tediously efficient and utterly insensitive man, anxious for his 2 per cent.

This was a travesty, of course, but one that filled me with disappointment. For me, the name Quancard had until then held quite different connotations: memories of my most restful afternoon at work.

Adnams used to buy several hogsheads of claret each year from Château de Terrefort, a modest Bordeaux property that belonged to the Quancard family. One of my earliest holiday jobs (while still at school) was helping to bottle this wine, and I decided on my first visit to Bordeaux that I should visit Terrefort. I tried to make arrangements through the *négociant*'s business, Les Fils de Marcel Quancard, quite unaware that there had been a row some years before, and that the half of the family which ran the business was hardly on speaking terms with old Jean Quancard who still lived at the château. The whole project was treated as if I were about to embark on a hazardous expedition into hostile territory.

Eventually I found my way to a large, unpretentious and shuttered house which had the air of having been half-asleep for the past century. There was no sign of life. I rang a bell, heard footsteps down a stone-flagged passage and the door was opened by a short elderly man whom I asked to announce my arrival to Monsieur Quancard. '*C'est moi,*' he said, and showed me round with great courtesy while making disjointed but entertaining conversation. 'They've gone off with the key to the cellar,' he muttered, and offered me an apple instead of the tasting that I had been expecting. As I was wondering whether I should be going he announced, in the most natural way, that he normally reposed himself in the garden at this time of day. Would I care to join him? He brought out a couple of deckchairs, arranged them in the shade of a tall cedar and, without further ado, sat himself down and went to sleep. The gentle snores of my host, the somnolent air of the place and the warmth of the spring day were irresistible. I, too, closed my eyes. An hour or so later I awoke, scribbled a brief note of thanks and stole quietly away, leaving Jean Quancard to his dreams.

This was Henri's father and it was here that Henri grew up. As he says himself in an autobiographical sketch, written for my enlightenment: 'Until the end of the war, Henri Quancard spent his idle life at the Château, essentially interested in catching fish and birds. No wonder one day he became a salesman.' So we, the poor customers, are his prey!

Henri's sketch continues with details of the hard work and study that formed the framework for his subsequent life. He learnt a great deal from visits to the growers with his father who also allegedly taught him that 'the best is just good enough for an English wine buyer'. From 1957 to 1964 he travelled in Germany and England as a salesman for his father (then a substantial shareholder in the *négociants'* business), while following weekend courses in business studies and administration. In 1964 Jean Quancard, under pressure from his brother, sold his shareholding in the firm and shortly afterwards had a heart attack. Henri had to sign an agreement with the other members of the family not to sell Bordeaux wine for five years. He went to Champagne and built up the French sales for an association of growers, but returned to Bordeaux as soon as the five years were up, in 1969. 'There he met the Prince of the French Wine Trade, Jean-Pierre Moueix, and that meeting finally orientated Henri Quancard's life.'

He became a *représentant multicarte*. This is one of those legally defined economic species, so typical of French commercial life. This type of functionary can represent several companies but no more than one from each wine-producing region (to avoid competing loyalties). He is paid by the companies in question, either on a pure commission basis or by a mixture of salary and commission. He has the exclusivity for the sale of their products in one particular market.

In Henri's case he is the UK representative of J.-P. Moueix (Bordeaux), Moreau (Chablis), Beauquin Santejean (Loire) and David & Foillard (Beaujolais and Rhône). But Henri has always had fingers in plenty of other pies, so he established his wife, Nicole, in business as a broker, dealing on a commission basis with a large number of producers from various parts of Bordeaux and elsewhere in France. What started (in 1977) as a technical arrangement to avoid fiscal problems became a reality, as Nicole acquired a zest for her job and worked at it almost as hard as Henri himself. 'Good business for Henri Quancard and his sons.'

Henri's habit, when writing these autobiographical notes, of referring to himself in the third person is typical of the continually entertaining mixture of attributes which form the basis of affectionate gossip amongst his clients. It reflects a similar aspect of his personality to the red-chalk drawing of the man which hangs in the hall of his (extremely grand) house in Bordeaux. The artist has given Henri an air of pensive nobility, like an idealized portrait of Napoleon. I pointed this out to Nicole once and she replied with a sigh, 'Yes, I always cry when I look at it. It makes me think Henri is dead!'

Like Napoleon, Henri is fond of hats. The one by which he was known for years was christened 'brushed fox' by Mark Lake, a merchant who specializes in old cognac and new mustard. It seemed impossible at one time to go anywhere around Bordeaux without seeing it skulking on the hat rack, announcing that its owner was already closeted in the inner sanctum with the man you had come to visit. For a while it was replaced by a strange thing made of blue denim, rather like a more substantial version of the floppy white sunhat beloved of English cricketers. It was too large for Henri, who peered out expectantly from beneath its brim. I was so astonished when I first saw it that I stood and gawped. Henri looked hurt, as he often does when trying to grapple with the English sense of humour, but it is hard to resist teasing him when he grasps so earnestly at the bait.

Henri's earnestness, indeed, is reflected in his almost relentless hard work, his reluctance ever to miss out on a possible deal. This sometimes leads him into errors of judgement, like the day he first took me down to Langon to meet Pierre Coste (a man wholly dedicated to quality). On the same morning he introduced me to the most unprepossessing firm of *négociants* I have ever encountered, a sharp and shady-looking bunch, selling purely on price. There was another day, a Saturday morning at the end of a hard-working week in Bordeaux, when Henri had persuaded me to go with him round some minor châteaux in Bourg and Blaye. Our first stop was at a farm that typified the worst level of uncaring incompetence. We were shown the filthy *chais* (wine storehouses) by the proud owner, an underfed man in a dirty mackintosh who was accompanied by a gangling youth, the '*maître*'; a dangerously surly lout who appeared to have escaped from a horror movie. The wine, filtered through cow dung, was *not* what I was looking for. Nonetheless I still see the name of this depressing property appearing on the labels of samples at the marathon tasting which Henri inflicts on me whenever I visit him.

He is, indeed, irrepressible. I came back to the Hôtel de Sèze one evening to find him waiting for me with a peasant grower from a co-operative in Champagne. Henri earnestly recommended this co-op's wine, and then asked me if the grower could join us for dinner! He himself was unable to come. 'It's Nicole's birthday,' he explained.

If he occasionally allows his salesman's enthusiasm to run away with him, Quancard's strength is that he does recognize quality, and that he understands his business. His alliance with Moueix was vital, for this is a company that never sold wine without the appellation (even in the days when their rivals were doing tremendous business on the English market by evading the legal controls that applied in France), and which always honoured the spirit as well as the letter of its commercial obligations. Jean-Pierre Moueix was, as Quancard rightly saw, a 'prince' in his profession, as well as being an art collector of renown and a man who defended the quality of the French language by the elegance and courtesy of his expression.

When Quancard started working with Moueix, they were simply one amongst a number of very successful big *négociants*. Then came the crash of 1973–4 when almost all of them lost money heavily and many either folded or were taken over, often with an injection of foreign capital. Moueix is one of the few major firms to have survived with family control intact, and to be still operating on much the same scale as before.

With the decline of one type of family business, others have emerged, based in the vineyards, with the necessary bank loans backed by the vital collateral of land. There has also been a development of the co-operatives and of the big independent *vignerons*, shrewd entrepreneurs who have often made money elsewhere. And, at every level, there has been an improvement of quality, coupled with a substantial increase in the acreage under vine.

The decline of the *négociants*, and the other structural changes in the Bordeaux trade, has been counter-balanced by the emergence of new, lightweight organizations like that of Hernandez. Henri is ambivalent about this development, having worked with and then fallen out with Hernandez. He talks about the success of such men being made 'from the work of generations of people who could not fight back any more when the crash came because they could not lower their overheads'.

But Quancard does see a trend towards more direct contact between grower and customer though he justifies the position of the *négociant* such as Moueix. 'They are growers, high-class vinification advisers to the growers, well-advised buyers and bankers to the growers. How could any modest functionary at any stage of the trade replace them?' There is, nonetheless, a considerable growth in *vente directe*, the direct sale from the château to the domestic consumer or foreign merchant. This is especially apparent in the lower appellations, where the depressed level of prices simply does not allow the grower to make a profit if he has to give the *négociant* his margin. But such changes are inhibited by the French taxation system which may reclassify producers who sell direct as *négociants*, thus losing the fiscal advantage of being farmers.

Nothing much is likely to change in a big way until the next crisis. 'When will that be? The factors now are international, not local. There is a larger and larger production of good wine, worldwide, but the consumption of red wine is not increasing as fast as white, especially at the bottom end of the market. If there is under-consumption there will be a crisis.'

Meanwhile, Henri does see the less professional *négociant* losing ground, especially in the middle section of the market. 'The broker has so much more information from a wider spectrum of buyers and sellers.'

Henri and Nicole Quancard have three sons. In a moment of dynastic grandeur he told me once that he hoped they would take over from him: one son could look after the English market, one the Dutch and German clients and the other could handle the French domestic sales. This dream is almost over. The eldest son is keen to enter the computer business and the youngest wants to be a chartered accountant. Only the second boy, Laurent, may end up working with Nicole, prolonging the family tradition. Henri claims to enjoy the 'cut-throat life' of the wine trade but he wants 'to make sure that if his throat is finally cut there is a survival.'

As I read these words in Henri's *salon*, Nicole comes briskly in, pulling on gloves, for they are going out to pick up the boys. The dramatic vision of Henri lying in a pool of blood, murdered by his competitors, is replaced by the reality of Saturday morning in Bordeaux. Henri's sons are not thinking about the wine trade – they are playing football.

Alex Wilbrenninck

Montreuil-Bellay is a small town due south of Saumur. It has a fine castle, perched high above the river, but this is not one of the famous châteaux and the river itself is a minor tributary, not the broad and lazy Loire that curls through the placid landscape of the 'Garden of France'. The town is a pleasant, sleepy place with a few tortured plane trees in the square, a number of old, but somewhat neglected, houses and the 'Splendid Hotel', named in this English style for some long-forgotten reason of deference or enticement.

If you walk down the street towards the hotel you pass on your left a rather grand stone archway, carefully restored, closed by a wooden gate. Lean over the gate and look in to the courtyard. It is a scene of peace and order. There are stone paths and low box hedges, edging neat plots of grass and flowers. Trained on the wall at the right are carefully pruned espaliered fruit trees, not a twig out of place. A fifteenth-century staircase tower breaks the line of the façade in front of you and is echoed by another, opposite, on your left. They rise into slate-covered points above the steep roofs of the house that encloses three sides of this courtyard. Beyond, not visible from the gate, is a walled garden and a tiny vineyard.

In the fifteenth century this peaceful and beautiful place housed one of the *sénéchaux* of the nearby castle, but when Alex Wilbrenninck arrived fifteen years ago it was a nearly roofless ruin.

He is a very remarkable man, a Dutchman from the province of Gelderland in the east of Holland. His family records show them living in the same area since about 1300 but Alex broke with tradition and moved, first to Heemstede near Haarlem (where he married Huubje) and then abroad. He was trained as an engineer and worked for the Dutch subsidiary of an American multi-national, General Electric. In 1967 General Electric took over a French company based at Angers and asked for French-speaking volunteers to go and work there. Alex and his family moved into an old, much decayed French manor house in the Loire Valley, and acquired a passion for the region, its architecture and its wines.

'At that time there were very few Loire wines exported, so my wife started sending bottles of wine from this region to friends in Holland, Britain and America. Our friends would come and stay with us for their holidays, and then they wanted some of the good wines that we enjoyed.'

Meanwhile Alex was promoted to the sales section of his company and for the next four years he travelled all over the Comecon countries of Eastern Europe, selling computers. More and more he grew resistant to the idea of uprooting himself, so when they eventually planned to send him either to the Middle East (selling computers) or to Spain (selling heavy engineering plant), he dug in his heels. Alex and Huubje decided that they wanted to stay in the Loire. Together with General Electric he planned his departure from the company, staying on for a year as a consultant to hand over to his successor.

Alex Wilbrenninck bought the ruin in Montreuil-Bellay and on 2 January 1972 he, his wife and four small sons moved into one room at the Splendid Hotel where they camped for the next six months. During the day he worked as an *agent commercial*, building export sales for the nearby Compagnie de la Vallée de la Loire (CVL), one of the first big wine suppliers to most English supermarkets, including Sainsbury's. He handled a few wines from other regions, particularly for his customers in Holland; and in the evening, he went to classes run by an ancient guild, where he exchanged his knowledge of accountancy for the skills of a stonemason. In every spare moment he rebuilt his wonderful ruin, largely with his own hands.

Everything was done in the original style, slowly and painstakingly. They moved out of the hotel and into the old stable, now the boiler-room, of the seneschal's house. A month later another room was ready, a dormitory for the boys, and slowly they expanded into the rest. It took nearly ten years before the last stone was in place and the last wooden peg hammered through the joint of an ancient beam. The result combines the structure of medieval France with the calm, well-ordered domesticity of a seventeenth-century Dutch interior, like a scene by Pieter de Hoogh. The portraits of Wilbrenninck's great-great-great-grandparents hang in the sitting room, approving all they survey. Garden implements, carpenter's and stonemason's tools are ranged neatly in their place in an outbuilding and the ancient cellars are excavated and filled with wine. The kitchen is particularly evocative of Holland, with wooden cupboards, every pot and pan gleaming in ordered rows, jars of preserves and a large, florid old clock, ticking quietly on the wall. It leads straight onto the courtyard through glazed doors that stand open for much of the year. This is the busy, peaceful centre of family life.

Above is Alex's office: a long, light and airy room, floored with small, ancient tiles, but filled with the gleaming paraphernalia of a modern business — telex, word-processor, typewriters and telephones. For while he restored the house and explored all the historic backwaters of the region, Alex was busy discovering the old cellars of the small growers and the modern warehouses of the big producers, promoting the sales of everything from simple *vins de pays* to the rarest treasures of the Loire.

In 1973 he established a new company with a university friend from Holland, a biochemist with a love of wine: Anton van Dijkman. They called it La Française d'Exportation. Alex looked after the supply part of the company, offering wines from all over France, while his friend organized the distribution in Holland.

Wilbrenninck continued to work with CVL, but his own business was expanding all the time. He was one of the early enthusiasts for the Buzet co-operative and he handles wine from Cahors and Madiran, Corbières and Minervois as well as his personal favourites, the wines of Bordeaux (especially Pomerol, Graves and Fronsac). But the basis of the business remains the Loire. Much of this was bread and butter stuff, the basic appellations, but Alex's own interests were always in the individual wines, from the smaller growers. One of his great coups was discovering the so-called 'secret cellar' of Moulin Touchais, a fabulous cache of old vintages of fine sweet Anjou, amassed by a vineyard owner and right-wing *député* who had the habit of selling only those wines which displeased him. There was bin after bin of old Anjou, going back to the nineteenth century, and it was Wilbrenninck who finally persuaded Monsieur Touchais to release these extraordinary stocks to the world.

He is a very persuasive man because he is trustworthy. Alex has done flamboyant things, like persuading a friend from the local flying club, Jean-Claude Etienne (his label printer), to pick up potential customers in England, whisk them over to the Loire for a day and dazzle them by low, swooping turns over the fabulous châteaux and the vineyards of this lovely region. But you know that these are not marketing stunts: they grow out of the man's genuine enthusiasm for his patch. 'The French are very difficult to do business with, but they have such a rich culture, history and language that these compensate for their weak points. In the wine trade, in particular, they are very nice people.'

So is he. This sense of decency is reflected in the harmony of his family life. I remember one evening after a long day travelling from one cellar to another, when we ended up at home in Montreuil-Bellay. Huubje was ill with 'flu, being nursed by one of their sons. Alex slumped exhausted into a chair, and the boy came in and quietly lit the fire, then went to stand behind the chair and massage his father's shoulders. This unspoken rapport and mutual trust is something that Wilbrenninck has transferred to his business life.

He no longer works with CVL but concentrates exclusively on his own company and recently, since an operation for cataracts in his eyes, he has decided to leave the mass market to his associates, and to deal only with the better wines.

I asked him why he had succeeded so well in France. His answer was curious: 'One thing that we do not have as foreigners is jealousy. The French *négociants* are very jealous of each other while the foreign merchants do not have that. They help each other, and often direct customers to each other. If I know that a friendly rival has a wine that I cannot supply I will not hesitate to say so. Many people find this approach very helpful.'

Indeed they do. Wilbrenninck does not always offer wines that I find attractive, but he does care and he works extraordinarily hard, offering a service which is unmatched by most of his competitors.

I am reminded again and again of the calm, tolerant, upright temperament of the Dutch; the impression of restful enthusiasm and bourgeois virtue, in the best sense of those words. The great age of the Netherlands, the height of its maritime power and extraordinary wealth, was in the seventeenth century. Other nations have expressed their golden age in flamboyant ostentation but the masterpieces of Dutch painting are mostly small-scale works, celebrating moments of domestic life.

IX
Town & Country: The English Merchants

Survival of the Fittest

Twenty years ago the independent English wine merchant was an endangered species. They had lived a charmed life for years, protected by legislation and custom which preserved a non-competitive, clearly defined structure of distribution that began with the London agency house and continued through the wholesalers to shops, restaurants and hotels. The consumer eventually paid a price that reflected the handling charges of a good many idle fellows along the way. Nobody ever went near the vineyards except to have a good lunch with the *négociant*, and all buying was done from samples 'on the slab' or on the recommendation of the trusted face who was selling to you. 'How can you possibly buy wine in France when it's going to be drunk in England?' was the view of one eminent City merchant.

There were exceptions, like Walter Berry, the highly successful head of Berry Bros, but most wine merchants of the 1930s were an unadventurous lot and the succeeding generation, coming back to the trade after the war, seemed lamentably ill-equipped to deal with the pressures of a rapidly changing world. They perished by the score when the climate of commercial life turned suddenly colder, and predators roamed the land.

The most fearsome of these were the big brewery companies, formed by a series of mergers in the 1950s and early 60s. They were intent on expanding their wine and spirit divisions by taking over or supplanting the wholesalers who had previously acted as their agents. And they also bought famous companies for prestige, destroying many a great reputation in the name of marketing.

Times became tougher still when resale price maintenance was abolished, and the supermarkets suddenly became a force to be reckoned with, using cut-price whisky and gin as a lure to bring in the customers. Their competition, and that from the trade 'cash and carries', pushed many of the smaller firms out of business.

Finally, there was a transport revolution which greatly favoured the larger companies at the expense of the local wine shippers. Even the small wholesaler used to buy much of his wine in bulk; a few hogsheads of claret, half-a-dozen 'pièces' of burgundy, some butts of sherry and a pipe or two of port. Bottled with simple equipment (or entirely by hand) and labelled with his own name, such wines gave the merchant a good profit.

But those leaky wooden casks could not be stuffed into a container or stacked on a pallet; they did not 'fit' into modern transport systems. So the hogshead was replaced first of all by something called the 'safrap container' (which held a great deal more wine) and this in turn was superseded by the road tanker. The smaller shipper couldn't handle this volume of wine in one delivery, and so he had to ship in bottle, glass and all. The cost of doing this became extremely competitive as handling systems improved and motorways were built, but again the system favours the larger importer. The economic unit is the 40-ft container which holds about 1,200 cases of wine. Smaller consignments cost very much more. As an extreme example, it is cheaper (per case) to ship a container of wine from California to Southwold in Suffolk than it is to deliver a single case from Southwold to the customer's door in London.

Unable to cope with these changes, many independent wine merchants went to the wall or were absorbed by larger companies. The smart London firms, who had lived so easily, were the first to succumb. Bypassed by the agency houses who went direct to their best customers, and struggling with ever-rising overheads as the competition for central London offices pushed rents and rates through the ceiling, they looked out of the window and saw competitors all around. Every road had a supermarket and the back streets were filled with cut-price off-licences, many of them belonging to short-lived chains that went bust with monotonous regularity.

In the country, by contrast, there were still rural backwaters where communications were poor and the population too sparsely

spread to warrant a great deal of attention from the larger companies. Overheads were lower and good service still counted more
than the last penny off a price. Above all, however, there were a lot
of determined individuals who had never accepted the dictatorship
of the capital, implicit in big business, and were not going to start
now.

One way was to band together to increase buying power and secure better discounts from the whisky distillers and other big brand
owners. The first such group was the Independent Wine Merchants
Association (later renamed the Merchant Vintners Company)
which was set up in 1965, specifically to counter the power of the
brewers. Today it has around twenty members, including some of
the country's leading wine merchants (Tanners of Shrewsbury, Lay
& Wheeler of Colchester, and my own company, Adnams of Southwold). The last-named was only admitted after a special vote to
rescind the Article of Association which banned the membership of
brewers.

IWMA was followed by similar organizations which united regional brewers, wholesalers and other groups within the trade: Clan
South, Leonard Tong, Forth Wines and so on. Terms of membership varied, but the aim of each group was to enable individual companies to share in aggregate buying terms which equalled those of
their largest competitors. The Merchant Vintners Company has
probably been unique in the extent to which it has developed joint
shipments of wine and has pooled buying expertise from rival companies, but even here the whole point of the exercise has been to
retain each member's separate identity, rather than submerging it in
a corporate whole.

Within these consortia are many companies whose turnover
relies primarily on the well-advertised national brands, sold at very
low margins of profit. They will remain vulnerable. Others, however, have seen that the most interesting (and profitable) development lies in the pursuit of quality, backed by a high level of service.
Of their nature, supermarkets and off-licence chains find it difficult
to handle the wines of small individual growers (often the best in
their region) or to give their customers the advice and service that
they increasingly require. By seeking out the very best, even if available quantities were extremely limited and shipping costs con-
sequently high, the regional merchant could offer his customers
wines which they would not find in the shops and for which he could

charge a modest premium, sufficient to cover a proper level of service and provide him with a decent living. Unlikely to attract the first-time buyer (the natural client of the supermarkets) they could, nonetheless, satisfy the novice who had discovered the anonymity of blended and branded wines and wanted something better.

All of this implied a great deal more work than heretofore, because the merchant had to travel to see the wine-growers and negotiate direct. He had to learn to speak foreign languages without embarrassment (most un-English)', and to master the paperwork of shipping, which vastly multiplied after Britain joined the Common Market. He had to produce an informative wine list and to maintain good relations with the increasingly influential wine writers. And he had to introduce his conservative staff to the benefits of computerization and other modern business methods.

To cap it all, the country wine merchant found himself confronted by a new band of eager competitors, partly stimulated by his own success. As the mergers of the big companies threw experienced wine-buyers out of a job, they increasingly set up on their own. Sometimes they acted as brokers between the growers and the trade, which was useful to the hard-pressed merchant who could thus benefit from their expert knowledge of particular regions. Frequently, however, they became traders in their own right. They rarely tried to match the range of the traditional merchants, but busied themselves with their individual specialities.

They were joined in this increasingly crowded field (mostly at the top end of the market) by a motley crowd of wine enthusiasts – amateurs who turned professional. Roger Harris developed a mania for Beaujolais while working for Peugeot; Robin and Judith Yapp somehow combined full-time jobs (as a dentist and doctor respectively) with the development of a top-quality business in wines from the Rhône and the Loire; Neville Abraham emerged from his business school background to set up Les Amis du Vin (not to be confused with the American organization of the same name). And there were many more.

Finally, this resurgence of individual, top-quality firms reached London. O.W. Loeb and Corney & Barrow were joined by a good number of rejuvenated traditional merchants and by specialist newcomers with a shop or warehouse from which they dispensed good wines and good advice to a more-or-less local clientele.

And *everybody* woke up to the fact that the good old International Exhibition Co-operative Wine Society (Chairman, Edmund Penning-Rowsell) had for years been doing tremendous business on a mail order basis, and that the cost of delivering a case of wine anywhere in the country was not necessarily any higher than the overheads incurred in operating a shop (and was, in fact, often less). So the country wine merchants and the London wine merchants went national.

There had been a moment when it seemed that the only people who were able to make money in the wine trade were the manufacturers (mostly distillers), the owners of successful brands, like Harveys of Bristol, or the fly-by-nights who engaged in fraud. Volume on its own was not enough because of fiercely competitive pricing at the bottom end of the market. Now it is widely apparent that there is another way to succeed: by the pursuit of quality. The field is over-crowded, and there are plenty who offer the same old substandard goods with more elegant descriptions (*caveat emptor*). But the revival of the independent wine merchant has meant that the fortunate consumer now has a greater choice of better wines than has ever been offered before.

Corney & Barrow: 'Plus ça change'

When Keith Stevens joined Corney & Barrow in 1936 at the age of seventeen he was, as they say, 'frightfully keen'. So he went to see the Chairman to get himself clued up.

'Uncle Charles, will you tell me about the wine trade?'

'Yes, my boy. If they don't want a second glass, the wine's no bloody good!'

'Well, the Stevenses never let the side down in that respect,' murmurs Geoffrey Jameson, Chairman of Justerini & Brooks.

Corney & Barrow moved offices a few years back from the heart of the City to an old rectory in Helmet Row, north of the Barbican. Yet the atmosphere hasn't changed very much. 'Will you wait in the drawing room?' asks the receptionist. There is a club fender ('given us by a livery company with whom we've been dealing longer than either of us can remember'), and the walls are hung with prints from *Vanity Fair*. A comfortable sofa and a couple of armchairs surround the coffee table, laden with coffee-table books, and the bottles on the sideboard indicate that most of the visitors drink gin and tonic or sherry. But the fridge, concealed in a cupboard, is full of champagne.

This is one of four London wine merchants whose history extends for more than two centuries; all of them are holders of the Royal Warrant. Robin Kernick (present Chairman of Corney & Barrow) is also Clerk of the Royal Cellars. At this exalted level, the sense of tradition and respectability can easily result in a certain inertia, stifling innovation. Berry Bros, the lordliest of this select group, has survived thanks to the royalties on the sales of Cutty Sark whisky in the States and the rent-roll from its valuable properties in St James's. Its grand customers tend to be too conservative to change their wine merchant, despite a noticeable failure to reincarnate the vinous expertise of the legendary Walter Berry. Christopher's, the oldest-established of the wine merchants (it predates 1666), was in continual decline until it sank into the embrace of Scottish and Newcastle Breweries, whose Newcastle Brown Ale has probably started more fights than most beers. Justerini & Brooks was taken over by United Wine Traders who made so much money from selling J & B rare whisky in America that they were able to buy up Gilbeys – owners of a well-known brand of gin, a fine château in Bordeaux and lots of valuable agencies. The result of the merger was much too tempting to survive very long. They fought off one takeover bid (from the Showering brothers, owners of Babycham) only to be gobbled up by Watneys in 1972. Not many people wanted Watneys Red, and the 'Red Revolution' became the biggest advertising flop in UK history. Watneys set another record, for the most expensive British takeover, when they were bought by Maxwell Joseph's Grand Metropolitan Group.

Corney & Barrow narrowly escaped the same fate. They sold out in 1961 to United Wine Traders and so, like Justerini's, ended up as part of IDV, Grand Metropolitan's wines and spirits division. Defending themselves from the Showering brothers resulted in a drastic reappraisal of resources. Two fine wine merchants in the group seemed absurd, so IDV decided to sell Corney & Barrow. In any case, Keith Stevens (whose grandfather bought C & B from the last Barrow) proved such a nuisance on the IDV Board that they were glad to be rid of him. So there was a 'management buy-out', initiated by Stevens but engineered by a much younger and more innovative man. 'John Armit made the new Corney & Barrow, there's no doubt about that,' says Robin Kernick.

Armit was emphatically *not* traditional wine trade material. For one thing he spoke fluent French (the result of a French stepfather and a year at the Sorbonne). For another, his innovative energy was flavoured with an indefinably raffish air that didn't fit the languid social style of the old London merchants.

But there *were* social contacts – he could hardly have failed to make friends at Oxford for he spent his three years there (and a large chunk of his inheritance) in considerable style. He attended one lecture and missed his finals, sending his tutor a telegram on the day: 'Sorry can't make it. Love, John.' 'I became serious later,' he says.

One of the Oxford friends knew the Stevens brothers: Keith ran Corney & Barrow; Peter, in the incestuous way of the wine trade, subsequently became chairman of Justerini's. So in 1962 the bright but unqualified Armit found himself working for C & B. At a loss to know what to make of him, they stuck him in their vast cellars under Gresham House – an acre of subterranean space (formerly the stables of Sir Thomas Gresham) which Corneys held on a fast-expiring 100-year lease at £500 per annum.

There was a locked cage containing the finest wines – 'marvellous old bottles that were only used for lunch'. John's main occupation was decanting these rarities for the directors, while trying to avoid the debaucheries of whisky-bottling day ('everyone got completely cracked') and the advances of middle-aged cellar girls in the dark recesses of the vaults. 'You pretty boy,' they cackled.

After six entertaining months, Armit was sent to France. Corneys were still dealing with the likes of Calvet and Cruse, so there was a lot of wining and dining and a few good friendships were started ('Anthony Barton was marvellous') but no real breakthrough to the buying pattern of future years. Then home again, selling in the City, helping to control the wine bars and grinding away in the office. This was the time that United Wine Traders were merging with Gilbeys to form IDV. 'They were my least attractive years in the wine business – I've never been an organization man,' he says, but John gradually took over the effective day-to-day running of the business. In 1967 he was made a director, and a year later Keith Stevens came to him with the proposition that they should join forces to start the new company, with Armit as managing director.

'It meant doing everything, negotiating the deal with Jasper Grinling (of IDV) and raising the cash. I went to see Evie Hambro.

He was a magnificent man: huge, the old-style banker. I wish that type still existed. He was a great wine lover, and I'd done some business with him and we'd got on well together. So I went to him one afternoon and told him the proposition. "Absolutely," he said, "We'll do it. I'll just get my partners in." It took five minutes – he told each of his partners how much they were going to put up, all on a personal basis. Keith Stevens put some money in and I raised a bit with the help of Samuel Montagu.'

John Armit was managing director of Corney & Barrow at the age of thirty. It sounds grander than it was. 'I saw every single order that went out and I signed every single bill. We were making a loss, on a turnover of £300,000.' But the contacts and the reputation of the company had survived.

'I made the decision that I would not buy in England. I spoke French, liked France and got on well with French people. So I started looking for sources of good wines. I'd always been a great admirer of Pomerol, and had the feeling that it wasn't really understood in this country, so my first visit was to Moueix, whom I'd never met. I had lunch with Jean-Pierre, who was at his peak then – a marvellous man. We got on really well, discussing painting, of course, and Rostand and John Donne.'

And wine. John Armit came away from that lunch with the exclusivity for Château Trotanoy, one of the finest of the Moueix properties. 'At that time it was so little known that I was able to buy a range of all the older vintages going back to the '61, not in huge quantities but between fifty and a hundred cases of each year, both for Trotanoy and La Fleur-Pétrus.'

In Burgundy, John set his eye on Leflaive, the most sought-after domaine of Puligny-Montrachet. 'I think it took five years to get in, writing, telephoning, sending lists. I never met Vincent [Leflaive] until he agreed to see me in Paris. I'm quite sure that it was a mutual interest in beautiful women that persuaded him to give me the lion's share of the wine he had available for England!'

Other agencies followed. Armit started dealing with Georges Duboeuf, renowned *négociant* of Beaujolais. 'Through him I got into the wine and food mafia of that part of France: Bocuse, Troisgros [both great chefs], Lalou Bize [the formidable co-proprietor of the Domaine de la Romanée-Conti].'

And so the list changed character and filled up with classic wines, though still dominated by the favourite regions of the traditional

English market. It became an extraordinarily smart production, designed by Bartholomew Wilkins (then a neighbour of the Armits) and written by John, with lively and informative notes on his latest enthusiasm. Corney & Barrow flourished, helped by the surging prosperity of their City friends.

It was a time of boom (in shares, property and every dealable commodity, including wine). The greed of the Bordelais encouraged them to demand ever-higher prices, even for the really dreadful vintage of 1972. But it was a nervous time as the bubble came close to bursting point, just before the oil shock of 1973–4 pricked the balloon, causing the collapse of all these speculative markets. I refused to buy the '72s but many wine buyers felt constrained to press on. John knew that things had got out of hand, but was in a difficult position because of his agencies with Moueix.

'I went to see Jean-Pierre and said that I know I have a moral obligation to keep buying from you, but I don't like the vintage and the prices are absurd. I will buy, but remember that I am doing you a favour.'

Others were less cautious. In early 1973 John encountered two major British buyers in the gentlemen's loo at Bordeaux airport. 'What are you doing about this vintage John?' they asked. In a spirit of mischief he replied, 'I'm buying everything, as much as I can get.' They took him seriously (and lost a lot of money), but John went back to England and wrote to his customers, telling them not to buy.

'Come the crash I said to Moueix that we can now buy so cheaply in London that I can't continue with you. They came back and we made a deal on the '73s and '74s to balance it all out – it allowed us to sell the '72s at a sensible price. They acted very honourably.'

After things revived (with the 1975 vintage) Armit persuaded Michael Broadbent of Christie's to devote a special auction to Château Trotanoy. 'I got Harry [Waugh of Harveys], Eddie [Penning-Rowsell] and Michael to come and have a tasting of a range of vintages of Trotanoy, and then we published their tasting notes in *Decanter*. There was a section in the sale catalogue about Trotanoy and the whole thing was a great success.'

Corney's got the agencies for a string of the top Moueix properties in Pomerol and St Emilion: La Fleur-Pétrus, Magdelaine, La Tour à Pomerol. 'I was always angling for the big one,' and finally Jean-Pierre agreed. 'The day that I got Pétrus was also the day that I told Jean-Pierre that I was leaving. It was my going away present to Corney & Barrow.'

He didn't leave altogether (John still writes the C & B list and advises on their buying) but it was a very dramatic departure. 'It was long enough. Turnover was up to £2 million and things were running well. Everyone has a fantasy about living on a tropical island, and I thought that if I didn't do it then I never would.'

So Armit wintered in Sri Lanka, wandered between England, Ireland and France, and finally ended up buying a house on another island: Majorca. He has a wine investment company, catering for a limited number of big, regular clients, but he has continued to scheme and dream.

'I've always liked bars,' he says. While still at Corney & Barrow he had the idea for a really good rock music bar, and started Dingwalls, with the help of various friends and partners. That turned sour as the actuality failed to match the original dream, so they opened Zanzibar (elegant, cool and much more fashionable). Dingwalls was sold and the same team started a small restaurant and then The Groucho Club, a meeting place for the sort of people who found Nick Lander's L'Escargot so congenial: film and television producers, publishers and agents; the denizens of Soho.

And for the future? 'Madrid next. What an amazing city! It's the only place in the world where the clubs don't actually open until four in the morning!'

Without John Armit, Corney & Barrow has continued to expand but seems to be reverting to its traditional character. The Stevens family, represented by a son-in-law, are still the major shareholders, and the other directors are well-connected to the rich City clans: Tony Weatherall is married to a Keswick (a mighty name in Hong Kong), and Richard Peat's family founded the accountancy firm, Peat Marwick. The salesmen may visit their customers by motor bike but tend to have double-barrelled names and turn up at all the smart society weddings.

Corney & Barrow make a lot of money out of Château Pétrus but they treat much of the rest of viticultural Europe rather cursorily. Their biggest successes recently have been in developing their own restaurants and wine bars in the City and through their association with Ernst Gorge, shipper of vast quantities of inexpensive wines to the supermarkets. The traditional side of the business flourishes but 'without John working for us full-time, we present a squarer image to the world'.

Robin Kernick, the present Chairman, has no doubt that the

company retains its flair. My own view is coloured by the depressing news that they have raised additional working capital by issuing new shares to the Whitbread Investment Trust, giving that offshoot of the famous brewers a 20 per cent stake in Corney & Barrow. Whitbread's offices are only a couple of hundred yards away in Chiswell Street; they may well be benevolent neighbours but the history of the brewers in the wine trade does little to encourage optimism. Robin defends the deal: 'The money was vital to finance additional stock and for the development of further wine bars.' He also hopes to supply rare wines to the Whitbread empire and to develop overseas sales through the brewery's international connections. In return, Whitbread's are apparently keen for Corney & Barrow to handle some of their fine wine interests, starting with Antinori in which they have a shareholding. This will be something of a shock to C & B who, until recently, listed only one Italian wine!

The present intention on both sides is not to increase the Whitbread stake, although circumstances could well change, especially if Corney & Barrow gets a listing on the Stock Exchange. They may retain their independence but the precedents are not encouraging.

There is certainly no sense of foreboding in their dining-room as we conclude an excellent lunch. Instead, Robin Kernick is at pains to emphasize how times have changed. While acknowledging that about half their business is still with the City livery companies and corporate dining-rooms he points to their growing mail-order business and claims: 'We don't reckon any longer that we're only a City wine merchant. . . . In the old days the people who came to lunch were pretty much a set mould. We get all sorts now.'

A faint flicker of pain registers as his eyes encounter my tie. He looks across the table for reassurance to Geoffrey Jameson, Chairman of Justerini's and erstwhile Master of the Vintners Company. Robin has talked of 'increasing competition at the top of the pyramid' and of the fine wine market being 'more and more difficult', but Geoffrey is encouraging. 'As long as the cake gets bigger (which it does all the time) there will always be a place for the jam; for us and Corney & Barrow and for Adnams.' He inclines his head with great courtesy in my direction. 'The carriage trade has declined but there is growth from the mailing list, by word of mouth. There's an awful lot of disposable income about.'

Robin agrees. 'A lot of customers who come to Corney & Barrow now would never have got past our office manager in the old days. The greatest pleasure is selling to a customer who's never bought before.'

A decanter moves around the table, a 'light' tawny port in deference to the weather. This too is an innovation.

In days gone by Keith Stevens would only have served an old vintage and demanded that his guests guess the year. 'In the summer vintage port is a joke,' exclaims young Adam Brett Smith, in a spirit of revolutionary fervour.

'But a very good joke,' says Geoffrey Jameson.

Tanners: 'Gone Fishing'

'Tanners only usually open branches where there's something to shoot or fish nearby.' Richard Tanner's mother made the remark as we drove south through the rolling Shropshire countryside. The previous day Richard himself had stopped the car on the top of a nearby rise to show me the view over the high valleys towards the source of the Severn. 'We hunt over all that country. I love these hills – I suppose I must know every field for miles in that direction.'

Richard Tanner is much teased for his hunting (he has finally forced himself to retire as Master of the South Shropshire Foxhounds) but the feeling for his locality is wonderfully strong, and is combined with a knowledge of birds and flowers that has enlivened many a trip through the wine regions of France and which surfaces in the most entertaining way in the pages of his wine list. Who else would digress from singing the praises of his own brands of sherry to note that one of their suppliers is 'like his late father, an expert on the many migratory birds that pass through the area. The Straits of Gibraltar being fifty-nine miles to the south, this is the shortest sea-crossing to and from Africa.'

The family portraits in Richard's hall and dining-room are mostly of prize-winning sheep, the Shropshire variety bred by his ancestors. There is record of Thomas Tanner, Bishop of St Asaph around 1730, but he seems to have been the exception to the generations of Tanners who farmed these hills. One such, E. Craig Tanner, was described in the *Hereford Times* of 1919 as 'a pedigree man to the backbone, a firm believer in the blood of ancient and established sound lineage, with respect to the animal and bird kingdoms – horses, cattle, sheep dogs and poultry'. Rather short, possibly bald (the cap hides it), holding himself neatly erect, Craig Tanner looks and sounds much like the Tanners of today.

But there was also the one who went to sea, William Tanner, who, on his retirement as sea captain in 1872, decided to keep himself supplied with grog by setting up as a wine merchant, in partnership with his brother Henry. Curiously enough this was the same year that the Adnams brothers also set up in partnership, as brewers in Southwold, wholesaling wines and spirits on the side. The firm of W. & H.E. Tanner prospered, took on the agency for the distribution of Worthington beers and gradually expanded its influence along the Welsh Marches. In 1936 the company took over Thomas Southam & Son, long-established Shrewsbury wine merchants, and with them their premises at Wyle Cop, home of Tanners to this day.

The family still tended to see themselves as 'gentleman' farmers first, wine merchants second. Richard's uncle, Frank, and father, Clive, ran the business together for years, but their interest in wine was intermittent. As Richard puts it, 'Father had a fit of keenness after the 1914–18 war but then hit the depression years and he joined up again in the next war.' Frank, like his nephew after him, was Master of the South Shropshire Foxhounds, more concerned about 'pirate packs' encroaching on his hunting grounds than about the latest vintage report. And his brother Clive went shooting and fishing. 'He participated in just about every country sport. He was an expert amateur naturalist and he played cricket for the Shropshire Gentlemen.' And in 1915 he survived a bullet through the head.

The business was trundling along like many other wholesalers of the day, secure in the apparently unchanging nature of the trade, a well-ordered line of distribution protected by resale price maintenance. 'We had a few pubs and the distribution agreement with Bass Worthington. When I first joined, my father kept rubbing into me the fact that the beer was keeping the wine business.'

But they were wine merchants, so Richard trained for a year with various other companies in the trade and then went off to France for seven weeks with Robin Crameri (now a Master of Wine, with Greene King), following the vintage. 'I borrowed an old van from my father and we picked grapes at Bourg and at Château Palmer. Madame Bollinger gave us a super lunch at Ay and helped to pushstart the van afterwards.'

Then it was National Service, first with the King's Shropshire Light Infantry and then commissioned into the Gurkhas. Six months in Malaya for the end of the Emergency were followed by 'a marvellous year in Singapore and Australia. I wanted to stay in the army, I thoroughly enjoyed the life, but eventually I got a letter from my father saying "if you don't come back the business will be sold". I arrived home in November 1959 and started work the next day, preparing for the Christmas rush. In January my uncle Frank died, leaving my father on his own. He made John Pullin [a cousin] and me directors and told me to run the wine side.'

There wasn't much 'wine side' to run. A nicely printed but uninformative list was backed by very modest stocks. Richard drew up a more attractive list, illustrated by maps, but he still had to ask his father's permission for everything he bought. 'I didn't get many trips abroad in the early days but I think now that you gain far more when you do go abroad if you've learnt what goes on in the business.'

Gradually he assumed greater control and he managed to acquire an assistant, Richard Hayden. 'He has been absolutely smashing. He is responsible for the cellars and the top wine accounts and the day-to-day ordering. We do all the buying together. I do the travelling and go to tastings, but we discuss it all together and he does all the German buying which doesn't interest me at all.' But despite being the driving force behind Tanners' increasing success, Richard was still not completely in charge. 'I was getting all the stick for what went wrong but I didn't have the overall authority to rectify matters. . . . My father once said "There's only room for one gentleman in the business and that's me!"'

Nowadays Richard refers to his father (who died in 1983) with considerable affection. 'He was a great character. He taught me to get the most out of life and to enjoy the countryside. We got on terribly well to finish with.' But in 1974 it got to the stage where Tanner had to tell the 79-year-old man that if he didn't put him in charge he would leave. 'He gave me the sack for about three days and then re-engaged me as managing director!'

And so the man who is the epitome of the country wine merchant finally took charge of his company. He is deceptive, a person easily underestimated.

For years I believed that he hardly went in to the office, but spent all his time hunting, shooting or fishing. On trips to the wine-growers he does little to dispel this illusion – turning up in a tweed suit and heavy brogues on the sunniest of spring days and insisting on sending telex messages to his huntsman from the remotest areas of viticultural France. At Jaboulet Aîné, in the Rhône, Richard's conversation with Louis Jaboulet revolves round Jip, a black labrador that he bought for Louis which initially proved too cowardly to hunt wild boar, while my first instinct is to investigate the remaining stocks of classic vintages and secure what I can for Adnams

His driving is that of a man who enjoys a rough gallop, and he tends to fall asleep while navigating, and in love when he's not. As we progressed down the Napa Valley one blonde Californian after another stole Richard Tanner's heart, until he met Janet Trefethen and switched his allegiance to brunettes. He gazed into her windswept face while she, oblivious to her conquest, explained the latest piece of high-tech equipment and talked about clonal selection. He is still a schoolboy in some respects. All this might lead one to suppose that the success of Tanners owed little to the efforts of its managing director. But of course this is an illusion.

Richard does indeed go hunting several days a week in the winter but he normally gets to the office by eight, and on hunting days it is even earlier. Once there, he works protected from all telephone calls by a vigilant secretary. 'Having the name of the firm they all ask for me – everyone wants to talk to me about their daughter's wedding or something, but it just isn't possible.'

His talent, a quite exceptional one, is to ignore non-essentials but to deal decisively with the things that matter. At a tasting you can see him scowl or wrinkle his nose at the dull wines, and then suddenly perk up like a pointer when he comes across something good. The same is true at meetings of the Merchant Vintners Company buying consortium: Richard will doze away through the tedious stuff but will make his point firmly on matters that count.

It is a habit of decisive action that continues to play a critical part in the prosperity of his company. The most severe test of this ability occurred some years ago when Richard Tanner was faced with a crisis that could easily have wrecked his business.

The wholesaling of beers and minerals was an activity that needed a lot of space but only brought in a marginal profit. After a period of expansion Tanners' cellars at Wyle Cop were bursting at the seams and it was decided to build a modern warehouse outside the town to handle the beers. It was recognized right from the start that the venture would only work with efficient use of modern handling systems and maximum flexibility of operation. At first all went well but then the local organizer of the Transport and General Workers' Union demanded union recognition (which would have led to uneconomic staffing levels and restrictive operating practices). Richard Tanner decided there was only one course of action.

'I had enough inside information to know that they really meant business – there was one ambitious man leading the others into it. So I got a firm of management consultants in to prove it was uneconomic to operate under union demands. They in fact proved it was uneconomic even as it was! So I got an industrial relations consultant and said that we had to close down this business and we worked out a plan, in top secret, that separated the beer business from the wine business.

'This was August and I wanted to give a tidy run-down to the licensed trade but I was pretty certain that the union man would take them out on strike and so I planned in the minutest detail for the picketing and everything else that in fact happened – the press releases, the letters of dismissal etc., were all organized.'

Richard approached the whole affair with the attitude of a military tactician and the zest of a small boy.

'I got all the wine vans away from the warehouse on a certain weekend, ostensibly to cart straw for me, and then I called an "O" group for all senior staff on Sunday night at father's house and told them what was going on. I kept them there until the pubs had closed! On Monday morning Richard Hayden and John Pullin saw to everything at Wyle Cop while I went into the warehouse at 8 o'clock and told them they would get generous redundancy but that we had to pack up beer wholesaling because it was uneconomic. Mineral water manufacturing would have to go because without the beer drays we would have no means to deliver it and our wine-bottling also went (because the team that handled the mineral waters also handled the bulk wine).

'The union man took them out at 4 p.m. and we were picketed, ten men on the gate. I went to work there every day with two or three loyal aides and held all the pickets there while our wine business carried on normally. I had tremendous fun! I had my "OP" in a stack of beer kegs and with a pair of field glasses I could see exactly

what was happening at the gate. I kept them up every night by feeding them false information on when a van was going to leave and by
Thursday morning they were looking absolutely shattered, sitting in
their cars listening to the radio. So I sent the van out.'

There was a chase, an attempt by the pickets to block the en-
trance at Wyle Cop, a minor collision.

'There was a big traffic jam, father was cursing them up hill and
down dale, and a police constable came to tell me that one of my
staff had rammed a picket's car.'

The strike gradually ran down. 'After a fortnight I agreed to go to
a meeting organized by ACAS [the Arbitration and Conciliation
Service]. We argued from ten until seven and the union eventually
climbed down. The men got very generous severance terms and the
union lost.'

Richard is at pains to stress that despite the *Treasure Island* style
of his narrative this was a serious crisis, critical for the company.

'We had to close the warehouse on economic grounds. If we
hadn't done it the way we did we couldn't have extracted the beer
trade from the wine trade and the whole company might have collapsed. As it was we were down to a tiny profit that year and we lost
a lot of business. But eventually it proved a good decision because
the reps were able to concentrate on selling wine, much more profitably than beer.'

Tanners have in fact grown steadily ever since. In 1978 they took
over Pulling & Co., Herefordshire wine merchants who had also
been distillers and had started, in the eighteenth century, as cider-
makers. 'Buying Pullings gave us a great surge. We are now wine
merchants from the Welsh Marches to the Cotswolds,' with a
bonded warehouse, three wholesale depots, eleven shops and a few
pubs, as well as a growing mail order business.

The heart of the company remains the wholesale side, selling to
hotels and restaurants in the region against the competition of other
local wholesalers, the big breweries and national wine companies.
Their very considerable success is attributed by all concerned, without any hesitation at all, to service. 'Service is the main thing – that's
top of the tree,' says Richard Hayden. 'I'll make sure you'll get anything the next day if necessary. Value for money and the length of
the list are important but service comes first.'

Richard Tanner agrees. 'I don't think one can hope to survive in
the wine trade unless you do everything very well, and sell every

way you can. Nothing remains static.' This is particularly noticeable with regard to the private customer. 'The old county trade is changing. Now many more farmers are buying in quantities just as big if not bigger than the old county people.' Richard Hayden is blunter: 'Most farmers in the old days drank whisky. Now they're drinking more wine and they've got plenty of money.' These, of course, are the men whom Richard Tanner meets all the time. 'You can never escape from it. That clay pigeon shoot I went to – the man whose land it was on wanted to talk about swapping some 1963 vintage port for some '70s.'

Tanners do not expect to get more shops ('they're very expensive in management'), but they are finding considerable growth in the mail order side, all across the country. Here again service is important, although, as Tanner points out, personal service to several thousand names on a mailing list is not really possible. 'You have to give the illusion of personal service': he does this by the use of very efficient and carefully thought out systems to process orders, follow up on complaints and so on. They use a word processor to produce personalized letters in response to standard enquiries, and computerization plays its part, but a great deal of record-keeping is still done by hand, with each customer's history of orders and problems available on file for immediate reference.

Throughout the business there is this attractive combination of modern ways of doing things with a distinctly provincial whiff of the nineteenth century. It is a combination which seems to make for contented customers, and Richard is clearly confident that his son, James (already a wine enthusiast), will be able to take over a thriving family business.

'Supermarkets and hypermarkets will introduce more and more people to wine. A percentage will become interested and will be open to the idea of going to a specialist, some becoming real connoisseurs. And the good specialists will attract these people. I think there's a great future for us.'

But at the same time Richard Tanner has thought about the limits to growth. 'We never have to ask permission from our bank manager for anything we do. . . . You can build a helluva rod for your own back if you grow too big.'

As you walk into the Wyle Cop premises with Richard Tanner at the beginning of another working day it is a bit like being on parade. It is a wonderfully old-fashioned place with a Dickensian front office, little changed for a century and a half, and a higgledy-piggledy complex of cellars and offices on varying levels that runs back from the street to the yard. Richard Tanner strides briskly through, greeting his staff and stopping here and there for a word. 'Morning, Mister Richard,' they say cheerfully as he pops his head into their tiny cubby-holes on his way to his own cubby-hole, hardly less tiny, upstairs. I asked him what he most enjoys. 'Difficult thing – I enjoy it all.' There was a long pause and then, knowing it sounded trite but confident that it was true, he said: 'I think I most enjoy running a successful business and seeing people happy.'

X
A Cautionary Tale

Steven Spurrier

*'Thurber's life baffles and irritates the biographer because of its
lack of design. One has the disturbing feeling that the man con-
trived to be some place without actually having gone there. His
drawings, for example, sometimes seem to have reached completion by some other route than the common one of intent.'*
James Thurber: *The Thurber Carnival*

Our hero was born with a silver spoon in his mouth (it may account
for the slight stammer), and has been one of the most innovative
people in his chosen profession, achieving fame while losing great
chunks of his fortune. Right from the beginning, Steven Spurrier
combined the ability to dream up one bright scheme after another
with the attractive but unnerving habit of forgetting about the bottom line.

Consider the facts. His family was from Derbyshire, prosperous
landowners enriched in this century by two successive inflows of
money. The first came about when a black sheep great-uncle was
banished to the village of Leyland for seducing too many local girls
and turned a modest bicycle shop into Leyland Motors, one of the
world's most successful manufacturers of trucks and buses. A fair
amount of this wealth was lost in the slump of the 1930s, but the
family coffers filled up again when Spurrier's grandfather dug a
gravel pit on his estate and won the contract to supply vast quantities of sand and gravel for the construction of Britain's first motorway. Grandfather eventually sold the business for £2 million in
1964, just as Steven was graduating from the London School of
Economics. At the age of twenty-three ('happily unemployed') he

was handed a cheque for 'an immense amount of money' and promptly entered the wine trade. Looking back on this decision, he sighs. 'I would have been much better off if I'd left my money in the bank!'

He joined Christopher's, the oldest wine merchants in London, and got them to send him (at his own expense) to Burgundy and the Champagne district. The next year he spent eight months in the wine districts of France, Italy, Spain and Portugal, 'learning masses and becoming completely hooked on good wines.' In Bordeaux, he remembers, the snobbish *négociants* took him out to lunch and dinner, plying him with old vintages and fresh gossip, while the two other trainees from Christopher's (without benefit of private incomes) had to be content with sandwiches in the cellars.

Spurrier then entered the firm of Murray & Banbury, 'an amazing company that had agencies for all the great estates (they even handled the Domaine de la Romanée-Conti for about fifteen minutes) but had no conception how to sell'. Steven felt very much at home there, but even he could see that it wouldn't last and he got out in 1967, a year before they went bankrupt.

He bought some land in Provence, got married and settled down to the idyllic life of a rural tax-exile, miles from the big brewers who were driving all the best wine companies out of business. After a couple of years, bucolic isolation began to pall, so he went to Paris and bought a tiny wine shop, the Caves de la Madeleine. It was owned by an elderly lady, who was appalled when she realized that the prospective purchaser was an Englishman. 'So I agreed that I would work with her for six months. If at the end of that period she felt I was not the right person I would leave it at that; otherwise she would sell me the shop. It proved to be an invaluable period. I learnt how to speak French, learnt how a shop works and what the French bought.' The period of apprenticeship over, Spurrier took charge on April Fool's Day 1970.

'It was a tiny, tiny shop.' People still came in with their six-star litre bottles for a refill from the tanks of bulk wine at the back. 'But I started changing the quality of the wines and holding tastings in the cellars. I wanted to open a wine-tasting room so when the place next door was on the market I took it over.' An American friend, who was wine correspondent on the *Herald Tribune* and had been giving wine courses in the local café, joined up with Spurrier to start the Académie du Vin, mostly for the English and Americans. 'It never occurred to me to teach the French about wine, but we got written up in the French papers so we employed a French partner and from 1973 we were giving the courses in French. . . . The French have now become very interested in wine but they weren't when I started. There were only about ten interesting wine shops in Paris, and they didn't even know about wines like Cahors and Madiran.'

The publicity was tremendous. An Englishman running the best wine shop in Paris was galling enough to the tender chauvinism of the French, without the added aggravation of starting a wine school. For foreign correspondents in search of a story it was a godsend. Notoriety and fame enveloped Steven Spurrier. But he was an Englishman, lacking the ruthless commercial instincts of the international entrepreneurs. Instead of capitalizing on his renown, he bought a vineyard in the Rhône and a restaurant down the road from his shop. Both proved financially catastrophic, and he compounded the bank manager's nightmare by a remarkably casual attitude to his real assets.

When a friend in England wanted to leave his boring job with a newsagents and go into the wine trade, Spurrier helped him set up shop in London, supplied him with his initial range of wines and allowed him to use the Caves de la Madeleine name. Anyone else would have regarded this as the start of a franchise chain and charged accordingly. Spurrier settled for 5 per cent. He was then approached by Neville Abraham, anxious to combine his business school background and wine enthusiasm (he was mad about Rioja). He mentioned to Spurrier that he lacked a name for his new company: 'Why not "Les Amis du Vin"?' suggested Steven, having registered this name for his own future use. A delighted Abraham concluded a deal whereby he had the name and Steven supplied him with wine for a year or two at a tiny commission. Abraham's next venture, the Café des Amis in London's Covent Garden, was largely modelled on Spurrier's pioneering Bistrot à Vin at La Défense in Paris even down to the logo, now that of the whole group. Steven's partner in this venture, Michael Liekerman, acquired a 20 per cent shareholding in the London Café but Spurrier himself ended up with only ½ per cent. Not surprisingly, he was less than enthusiastic when Abraham's expanding empire moved into wine education with the École du Vin, bearing a passing resemblance to Spurrier's own Académie du Vin in Paris, and the wine courses that he had organized in London in association with Christie's, the auctioneers.

The best example of Spurrier's promotional talent (and absence of commercial follow-through) is the famous blind tasting held in Paris on 4 May 1976, comparing top California wines with their French equivalents. There had been similar events before, but none which combined such a remarkable selection of wines with a panel of judges of unimpeachable expertise. All French (Spurrier's own marks were not included in the result), they included the head of INAO, several renowned growers and a couple of the top wine journalists.

The event was designed as an inexpensive, newsworthy way of gaining publicity for the Caves de la Madeleine in American Bicentennial Year and it was expected to have a particular result. 'I intended to rig it so that the French wines would win. That's why I put in Haut-Brion, Mouton and so on.' The prestigious *Guide Gault-Millau* was offered exclusive coverage of the event and accepted but (more prescient than Spurrier) panicked at the last moment. So Steven's American associate, Patricia Gallagher, rang up her friends on *Time* and the other US journals, and it was they who announced to the world the astonishing result. For the Californian wines 'won', overwhelmingly, in every category.

There was total silence in the French press about this affront to national pride but the gambit had extraordinary international repercussions. It came at a moment when the world was ready to be converted and, more than any other factor, it was this that put California wines on the map, not only for European consumers but also in the States where 'domestic' wine had previously been considered inferior by almost everyone except a few West Coast enthusiasts. As a publicity gambit for the Caves de la Madeleine it was of negligible import, but it transformed the California wine industry.

In France they didn't want to know. 'I was the first person to sell top-class California wines in France but I don't any more because the price is too expensive [a matter of exchange rates]. It was always a terrific hassle to bring them in. The French are unbelievable in this way – making every possible difficulty. One time when I had taken a great deal of trouble to get all the paperwork right the customs officers still wouldn't release the consignment. I rang them up to find out why. "We don't know where the wine comes from," they said. "But it says clearly on the papers and on the labels; it's from California," I retaliated. "We know that, but where is California? If a wine from

Burgundy goes abroad they have to say 'Produce of France' on the label, even though the whole world knows where Burgundy is." I had to print stickers saying "Produce of USA" and go down to the docks and put one on every single bottle before they allowed it out!'

It was Geoffrey Roberts, not Steven Spurrier, who really capitalized on the surge in interest in California. He signed up all the top wineries (including Mondavi) and sold a lot of California wine in England before the dollar exchange rate turned against him. Then he sold out to Spurrier's *bête noire*, Neville Abraham.

Now, after a brief foray in New York, Spurrier's commercial base is England. He has written a couple of wonderfully practical guides to the wines of France and he is helping to resuscitate the battered remains of the Malmaison Wine Club. This mail order business was started by Clive Coates when he ran the wine division of British Rail. He left when his bosses got cold feet about the enormous investment in stock and joined (somehow it seems inevitable) the growing empire of Neville Abraham, who also acquired (not through Coates) the Malmaison mailing list. The club itself (a trading shell) was sold to a bright wine trade entrepreneur called Graham Chidgey who later persuaded Steven Spurrier to work for him, which meant Steven was earning a salary for the first time in his life.

Today he looks back on the French wine trade (in which he is still involved) with considerable detachment: 'In the French wine business they make huge profits to compensate for the mistakes they know they're going to make. Rents are high, the telephone is high, wages are high and you have to pay 60 per cent social security on top of the actual wage. So you need a *minimum* of 50 per cent mark-up on cost just to cover your overheads.'

In practice the archaic chain of distribution often includes a *représentatif* between grower and shop who takes 10 per cent for doing nothing (sometimes never going near the vineyards), and there are absurd legal constrictions which ensure the survival of the middlemen.

'As a retail wine shop I am not supposed to sell more than 40 litres of wine or 3.5 litres of spirits to any client in a single transaction. I ignore it and they threaten to close me down. I tell them to go away: "You want ten people out of work?"'

But even now the system survives.

'You can have a grower in Burgundy send his wine to a *demi-gros-*

siste [wholesaler] in Paris whose cellars are in Bercy. He has his salesman who goes to the cafés and shops selling at a minimum mark-up of one third on cost plus a transport charge from the cellars. The retailer will take a minimum of 50 per cent on cost and then charge for delivery, even inside Paris. If it leaves Burgundy at 20 francs a bottle it may end up costing the consumer 50 francs, by the time you have paid VAT and transport.

'So you have this enormous competition from the *vente directe* sales, straight from the vineyard. If you jump into your car and head south you can buy the wine from the grower at maybe a franc or two more than the price paid by the wholesaler or the shop which deals direct. So the customer thinks I'm a complete robber if his 24 franc Sancerre sells in my shop at 36 francs, little caring that elsewhere you will have to pay up to 48 francs. . . . But at least the mail order *vente directe* is less important than it was, since it now costs 75 francs to deliver one case of wine from Bordeaux to Paris.

'If only you could trust the growers not to sell to your clients direct, but you can't. A potential customer will come into the shop, note down all the names on the labels and go hareing off down the motorway. Monsieur Guigal thinks I've sent him a friend and sells him a case out of my tiny allocation. At least you don't have that problem in England!'

Sitting in the Malmaison cellar, a railway arch below St Pancras Station in London, Steven Spurrier is still scheming away, optimistic and innovative despite the setbacks of his commercial life.

'With wine consumption in England expanding at 10 per cent a year there are bound to be greater opportunities for anyone who's alert in the wine trade.

'We have to bank on the individual store, offering more than just wine – perhaps books, glasses, and so on. You have to offer a range of services and give the customer the feeling that they are buying individually chosen products of impeccable quality, without any problems.

'People are going to spend much longer buying wine, treating it as a leisure activity. When you think of the disposable income that is spent on handmade shirts, shoes etc., wine seems one of the least expensive items which can enhance life in general. People will discriminate more. If the wines we sell are the best and perceived as such we shall be okay.

'We are not selling to the first-time wine buyer but to perhaps

5–10 per cent of the wine market because we are asking for much greater effort. But I should like personally to buy everything at a shop like La Vigneronne [see page 127]. It hits a need. It filters the case lots from the auction market through to its public. It's a complete treasure trove of things.

'In America, especially New York, people go wine buying at weekends – isn't it amazing! That might happen here.'

Steven Spurrier has been described by Hugh Johnson in Steven's book *French Country Wines* as a man who can't make up his mind. Perhaps because his mind is so full of different ideas. But his final conclusion on his profession is this:

'When I do finally make money out of it, I might even leave the wine trade and just buy the stuff for my own consumption.'

XI
A Nation of Shopkeepers

The Brewers v. The Rest

When the brewers destroyed the traditional wine trade in the 1950s and 60s, leaving a few fossilized survivors like Berry Bros, they must have been confident that they could persuade us all to drink the vinous equivalent of keg beer; treated to produce a neutral, stable and cheerless beverage, lacking the unpredictable individuality that makes wine interesting to so many people. They almost succeeded but were defeated by two things: the upsurge in demand for good wine in all its confusing variety (and good beer, good bread, fresh fish etc.) and the great leap forward of the supermarkets.

The revival of *taste* (consumer-led, to a great extent) was a matter of interest to a limited number of enthusiasts, at least at first, and it was largely overlooked by both brewers and supermarkets whose eyes were fixed on the dazzling statistics which showed an enormous expansion of the wine market as a whole. Consumption doubled or trebled (admittedly from a very modest base), and many believe that it will treble again, to the German level of thirty litres per head, per year.

The brewers' response was 'The Brand'. The brand made life easier for everybody (none of those complicated wine names to cope with) and the brand-owner gained all the benefit from the enormously expensive advertising campaigns because it was his name and nobody else's. Marketing men were kings of the new regime. Roger Holloway's most notable achievement before running Bass Charrington Vintners was to double the size of the British toothpaste market by discovering that people bought toothpaste to make their mouths feel fresh rather than to clean their teeth. From toothpaste he moved on to Mateus Rosé, which everyone bought because they couldn't decide whether they wanted white or red, sweet or dry, still or sparkling and anyway they could always make a lampstand out of the pretty bottle. Sales dropped when every other household in Britain had a Mateus lamp.

The supermarkets' answer was price. They started by selling the brewers' and distillers' brands as loss-leaders to bring in customers for the groceries and then discovered 'own label'. Without having to bear the brand-owner's advertising costs, own-label wines could be sold even cheaper and yet show a modest profit. But there was still the problem of all those *names*, so they concentrated on a few of them and turned things like Liebfraumilch and Anjou Rosé into generic brands. The sweet-toothed English were eager to be convinced that grape-flavoured sugar water with a Germanic label was actually quality wine.

Today the supermarkets control over half the British wine market. They have several things going for them apart from price: the convenience of one-stop shopping with car parking nearby; customer 'throughput'; a reputation for decent quality. This last was a spill-over from the grocery side of the business, hardly justified at first by the intrinsic value of their own-label wines. But gradually things improved and they have progressively moved up-market. The interesting range offered by Waitrose and the development of the Sainsbury Vintage Selection should give pause for thought to those who believe that the supermarkets cannot compete with the specialists.

Indeed, there is no reason why supermarkets should not offer the range of a delicatessen and the wine choice of a top merchant, as well as cookery equipment and books on food and wine. There is a continuing trend to improve quality (witness the installation of fresh pasta machines in a number of supermarkets), while retaining the classless appeal that is so important an element in their success.

Such an appeal is completely lacking in most brewery-owned multiple off-licences. Quite the reverse, these dreary places have the sleazy male-orientated image of the betting shop, wholly unsuitable when you consider that most purchases are made by women, on their way down the High Street between Habitat and Mothercare.

Many of these multiple chains are in decline, losing out not only to the back-street off-licences, family owned and open all hours of day and night (competition that a chain can never counter) but also, to an even greater extent than in the past, to the supermarkets. They have intrinsic disadvantages apart from their scruffy image. No parking, unexciting wines and high staff costs are the most serious. Staffing especially is a nightmare. You either employ uninformed assistants at low rates, or you train and pay properly, only to find that the manager who has passed his Wine and Spirit Trade Education Trust Diploma is bored selling quarter bottles of gin to old ladies and depressed at the poor value of much of what he has to offer.

Doubtless, the multiple chains will spruce themselves up and will survive, since they are backed by companies with huge resources. At present they seem set for a bloody and inconclusive battle to gain market share, a contest that will do little more than diminish the already pathetically low profit margins of the wine trade.

There is a way out of this impasse through the development of multiple wine-warehouses, staffed by well-trained and committed managers, able to offer tastings and other services and to stock an interesting range, while providing the hassle-free shopping that results from adequate car parking. With out-of-centre sites, rates per square foot will be lower and, with larger sized units, management costs more acceptable. The problem, however, is that such warehouses are not particularly suitable for the promotion of brands, since the customer who buys by the case has, one hopes, moved beyond the stage of drinking Blue Nun.

The future of brands and their rationale is, indeed, something so contrary to my instincts as a wine merchant that I had best not comment on the subject in any detail. Suffice it to say that brand promotion will continue to enrich the advertising industry and that there will be a widening of the range of brand-owners. The whisky distillers will probably follow the cognac producers into the wine market and will be joined in battle with Suntory and the other Japanese giants. All of which will put increasing pressure on the brewers.

What brands *have* achieved is to broaden the base of the wine market by demystifying wine for the consumer. The same is true of the wine box and other non-traditional forms of packaging. The box is relatively expensive (more so than the equivalent number of bottles) and comes out less well in blind tastings than the available alternatives. Nonetheless, it does represent a way of breaking through to the novice who may be so confused by the mystique of wine, even to the point of being subconsciously afraid of the class implications of the traditional glass bottle. The box of wine is simply a package, devoid of social implications, and it reduces wine to the status of just another beverage, like orange juice or milk. This is even more important than its much-touted 'convenience'.

But there are limits to the growth in sales of these alternative packages, whether box, tetrapack or can. They have to survive against a wonderful, recyclable device; ecologically acceptable, qualitatively unmatched: the glass bottle.

The traditional corked bottle doesn't simply encapsulate wine; it is the only package that enhances the quality of what it contains. That is of no great concern in the mass market (there is plenty of evidence to show that most wine is consumed within a fortnight of purchase), but it is of vital interest to the independent specialist, the top-quality merchant.

It is increasingly clear that well-run, individual businesses will survive and prosper. They can offer better wines, a better range and better service than either the supermarkets or the multiples, and thereby justify a better price. Their customers will rarely be first-time wine buyers but they can satisfy the person who has already discovered wine and wants to move on from the decent reliability of the big companies to the individuality and variety which is provided by the limited production of the top growers.

There is a great desire to learn (witness the explosion in the sale of cookery and wine books), and the combination of increasing wealth and increasing leisure gives the new generation of wine enthusiasts the occasion and the opportunity to 'browse'. They may browse through a well-written and well-presented mail order catalogue or they may wander round a well laid-out wine warehouse or shop, stopping occasionally for a chat with knowledgeable staff. In any case, they need to be able to feel that they have discovered a wine for themselves, while having sufficient guidance to help them through the confusing mass of names. Ultimately it is the quality of what they buy that will send them back again and cause them to spread the word amongst their friends.

La Vigneronne

The sign over the door says 'Wines, Beers, Spirits', and, at a casual glance, it looks much like any other off-licence. When you go in the door the first thing you see is a large bird cage, perched above a couple of old corking machines. In the cage is a very sleepy green parrot called Charlie, 'or maybe Charlotte'. And behind the counter is Liz Berry, Master of Wine.

So this is not another branch of Gough Brothers or Arthur Cooper, the High Street multiples, though some customers don't seem to notice the difference. While I was there last a girl wandered in from the street, bought a can of Heineken and left, without a glance at the bottles of vintage cognac by the door, the racks of claret going back to 1904 or the thirty-five vintages of sweet Bordeaux, from 1895 to 1982. If she had stopped to pick up a catalogue, she might have been intrigued to find wines from Bulgaria, Greece, Austria, Lebanon and Israel listed on the same page, following a lavish range of classics from California and Australia. I could go on, for this is a fascinating list (what is one to make of Monumento Rosé from Portugal?) but there isn't space to include it all. Indeed it is hard to see how they squeeze this amazing assortment of unusual bottles inside what is a very modest shop.

'It used to belong to Vincent Foods, the Europa supermarket group. It was the beginner's shop – it had the worst staff because it was the smallest of their wine shops.'

Now it has some of the most informative and best qualified staff in London. 'The manager has the wine trade Diploma with Honours, the other girl is half-way through the Diploma and the new chap used to work for the Canadian Liquor Board and starts the Diploma in the new year.' And there is Liz Berry herself, ex-teacher of classical guitar, and her husband Mike, ex-banker. Liz joined Vincent Foods on a temporary basis and ended up as wine buyer. 'I happened to be working in one of the licensed supermarkets, on the wine side, and they sent me on a wine course. I got hooked.'

That was in 1971. In 1980 Liz passed the Master of Wine examinations (the British trade's highest qualification) and in 1981 she started La Vigneronne. 'I had been saying to Vincents for several years that they should turn this into a fine wine shop. They didn't want to, so they sold it to me instead. We got a bank loan. We had to buy the existing stock but Vincents allowed us to run it down a bit first and gave us good terms to pay for it. We had about £5000 left over to buy stock – it wasn't very much. So we gradually bought a case here and a case there and we added a few wines from Mike's private cellar. After six months' trading, Mike left the bank and came in full time.'

Most of their wines still come from London merchants and from the auction houses. But these days they also buy quite a number of rarities direct from private customers, many of whom are referred to La Vigneronne by the auctioneers because their lots are too small to be catalogued or they want immediate payment.

I mention the problem of the variable condition of some of the older stock bought at auction. 'We make discreet enquiries about the provenance of stuff that we're interested in, and if we don't know where it's come from we generally cost in a bottle to taste. If we don't like it it goes back into auction or we sell it off as bin ends. . . . If a customer complains we will refund but we want the bottle back (with its contents) as soon as possible after opening. It doesn't happen very often.'

More and more, Liz and Mike Berry are importing direct. They make about six trips a year to France and ship small quantities from individual growers. This amount of travelling may seem a high overhead for a small shop, but Liz is confident that it is worth it, apart from the fact that they go together and do it for fun. Are they keen on food as well as wine? 'Unfortunately yes!' Liz looks down at her stomach. 'We're working our way steadily through the Michelin. Especially in the smaller places the restaurants often list things that you might not otherwise come across. We find a lot of wines that way, and by word of mouth from other growers. I'm particularly enthusiastic at the moment about the Alsace wines of Marc Kreydenweiss because he's our latest discovery. His was a wine we happened to have in a restaurant. We thought it was very nice, found his cellars at Audlau and spent most of a Saturday there talking to him.'

These and other discoveries are introduced to the customers of La Vigneronne at a series of tutored tastings throughout the year – nearly two a week, for between forty and sixty people each time. Liz and Mike Berry introduce the wines at about a third of the tastings and they haul in various wine trade friends to tutor the rest. Ticket prices vary between about £5 and £15 per head, and Liz is adamant that even the journalists, who give her exceptionally good coverage, have to pay 'with their own hard-earned cash'. She relents sufficiently to invite them to one or two free tastings each year and keeps them informed through the mailing list.

'We do a bit of mail order but about 50 per cent of our customers are local.' The shop is open until 11 p.m. each day (10.30 on Sundays). It must be quite startling for some of the late night partygoers to stumble through the door into this cave full of treasures, not to mention the parrot. In addition to delivery and glass hire they will decant old bottles for personal callers, advise on suitable wines for particular dinner parties, prepare special gift packs, provide tasting notes on their stock and search out rarities on request. And they take credit cards!

No wonder they are famous, despite the unremarkable exterior and the cramped lack of space inside. 'I might move to somewhere bigger eventually if the rent here got ridiculous but I don't want to open any more shops – this works because it's personal.'

What about selling food as well? 'We do a few French specialities – pâtés, foie gras, various tinned soups. It's all tins or jars rather than fresh. I'd love to do cheese, charcuterie etc., but there's a lot of wastage – and a lot of skill in the buying. There just isn't enough time. Our future lies in buying more of our wines abroad.'

Twenty years ago that would have been a revolutionary statement for a good many English merchants and it's still rather surprising for a small off-licence in the Old Brompton Road. If La Vigneronne inspires others to do likewise it will add enormously to the fun of going shopping. But I hope that they won't all stock parrots.

W.H. Cullen: James Rogers

Cullens was, until recently, a family business (despite being a public company since 1949). They started as grocers in Islington in 1876 but were selling alcohol by the turn of the century, and had built up a chain of a hundred licensed grocery shops in south-east London by 1920. Things flourished until the 50s and then, like many similar companies, they hit the doldrums. Everyone else was getting bought up at the time, and there was no particular reason for Cullens not to follow suit, except for a persistent sense of family loyalty. They survived, opened their first specialist off-licence in 1968 (just after the abolition of resale price maintenance) and eventually added a couple of wine warehouses and started a mail order business. Just as the losses were becoming hard to bear they found themselves caught up in one of those periodic bouts of takeover fever that seem endemic in the off-licence business. Towards the end of 1984 three prospective suitors emerged, backed by considerable finance from the City, and embarked on an extremely expensive courtship of the ailing bride. To the astonishment of many in the trade, the family was eventually able to pocket the best part of £8.5 million.

Since the takeover there have been drastic changes. Most of the wine shops have been sold and the group is in the process of reorganization. The picture that follows must be seen in this context; a matter of historic record rather than current reality. It is the portrait of an idiosyncratic company in the last days of family control.

Cullens was a series of paradoxes: a company firmly rooted in the nineteenth century that was, everyone agreed, consistently innovative; wildly old-fashioned and apparently inefficient but describing itself as Britain's most progressive; listed in the telephone directory with a string of shops, warehouses and offices but impossible to find.

The headquarters of Cullens' wine business was indicated on their stationery as being in Battersea Park Road, but if you wanted to see James Rogers you had to persuade the company to reveal the real location nearby, a completely unmarked warehouse next to . . . somewhere else. This curious desire for secrecy was apparently based on fear of attracting thieves.

So, late in 1984 I finally spotted a Cullens' van parked in a loading bay and squeezed past it to the door, climbed upstairs through a rabbit warren of warehousing, stuffed with stock, and emerged (somewhat dusty) at the top.

Here are the offices, crammed five-high with labouring minions, half-hidden by a haze of cigarette smoke. There are piles of paper everywhere, and the office furniture looks as if it was bought in a clearance sale fifty years ago. Here and there, not much in evidence, is the odd computer screen, visible symptom of the newly installed system which is competing against the accumulated book-keeping methods of a century past, known to initiates but impenetrable to others. The odds seem overwhelmingly in favour of inertia.

Nonetheless, in the smallest office of all, in the midst of these external signs of archaic immobility, sit two people (non-smokers) who manage to give out a convincing air of knowing what's going on. Paul Tholen, Master of Wine, has recently joined from another old-fashioned company, Greens, the City merchants. His job is to administer Cullens Wine Club, the mail order side of the business. His boss, talking to a supplier on the telephone, is James Rogers.

His great-grandfather founded the business, and a great deal of the recent reputation of Cullens is directly attributable to James's arrival in 1970.

'After leaving school I taught in South Africa for a year; Latin, English and sport. Then I came back and decided to be an accountant. Accountancy; abandoned. Bored and purposeless at that stage. So I gave that up and started in the business in 1970, working in the cellars. I was twenty-two.

'Father ran the wine side before me, and the other half of the family looked after the grocery business. It was a bit tense when I arrived – people were a bit guarded and were out to pick holes in me. We were totally in the shadow of the grocers and the shops came under the grocery section. Until eighteen months ago we had no professional wine people running the shops.'

Alcohol still only accounts for a third of turnover, but it is clear that James now runs the wine business with a fair degree of autonomy. His father's cousin is managing director of the company as a whole.

'When I arrived we were a classically-run small wine merchant, with a lot of French and colonial wines and nothing from Italy. Our house Spanish was Rioja and we sold a lot of Moroccan red, Sidi Larbi!' Sainsbury's were flogging the same stuff at 38p per bottle.

But James Rogers did have an important lesson drummed into him at an early age which he never forgot, despite the wastrel years. 'It was at the age of thirteen, when I was first allowed to stay up for dinner. My father said to me, "If you want to learn about wine, taste blind. You'll make a fool of yourself all your life, less as you grow older, but you'll end up knowing more than most people."

'We mostly drank wine from the classic regions, but when I joined Cullens my gut feeling was for the family business and wine was secondary. One wine changed me into thinking it was a very interesting subject. I tasted it blind. It was Viña Ardanza [a classic Rioja]. I couldn't believe it.

'It was a quarter of the price of the French equivalent. It was a turning point from a commercial point of view and set the standard for one's buying pattern which is, taste blind, otherwise you get preconceived ideas. I am totally anti-fashion with regard to drinking for names. If I can be different, with a reason, I'll be different.

'If I have twenty red wine samples in the office I get someone to pour them out into twenty glasses. I go down the row tasting each glass and I put a retail price on the taste. Then one looks at the twenty cost prices and the margin you want to make and decides accordingly.'

Any system has its drawbacks. You may taste twenty wines from different regions without a basis of comparison for any one of them. Some wines are 'show wines' – the type that exhibit an immediate appeal in competitive tastings, but which may be less interesting when you drink the second glass at table. A blind tasting that included a hefty Australian red and a classic Médoc would leave the Bordeaux wine's complexity of appeal overwhelmed by antipodean force. And the type of blind tasting outlined above has a certain haphazard nature – it may not give the buyer a proper chance to compare and select the best wines of a particular region or to assess an attractive sample against existing purchases.

But James Rogers' system *has* resulted in an interesting and varied list (he is a very gifted taster), and he is emphatic that he compensates for the systematic defects by doing 'parallel' tastings of different wines from the same region and that he does make allowances. 'If I come across something in one of my blind tastings that smells obviously big, I'll leave it till after, to try and get things in balance. I believe that smell is 90 per cent of taste – it's immediate, a quick comparison. If I'm tasting sixty ports, for example, that's very helpful because the palate simply couldn't cope. . . . Buying this way I find it does help your blind tasting enormously.'

The Cullens range includes some fairly esoteric wines (a good selection from Chile, for example, and plenty from Australia), but I'll bet that the Mouton Cadet wasn't selected blind. It is clear from reading the list that the wines are chosen primarily from samples supplied by agents and brokers in England, rather than from visiting the vineyards. James Rogers claims that the Australian and New Zealand wines resulted from a month's visit to the wine regions, but admits that in general he does not travel to investigate the latest technology of vinification or to knock on doors in the sleepy wine villages of Europe. He argues that 'there just isn't the time because in my business I have so many other things to do apart from the buying, and anyway the selection from the Continent that is offered me over here is very good'.

They operated a mixed bag of outlets. The grocery side was experiencing problems due to supermarkets moving progressively up-market and parking problems becoming greater. 'We don't get the same throughput as the supermarkets; we're convenience grocers rather than main-stop shopping stores. But one does have a very wide view of the wine trade. There are five major ways of buying wine: the grocer/supermarket; the off-licence wine merchant; wine warehouses; mail order; the auction rooms. We cover four of those five avenues.'

It's a question of putting your eggs in every available basket. James admits, for example, that Cullens Wine Club was started because he saw the success of the Wine Society and the *Sunday Times* Wine Club, and couldn't bear to think of them grabbing any of his own potential customers. But such an approach has its drawbacks, a dilution of effective effort and a 'fragmentation of the company's image' of which Rogers is well aware. It may be that in the future they will consolidate more on their strong points.

'I think wine warehouses are the best way to combat the supermarkets. You're getting the man and wife together, giving them the opportunity to taste and mix their case, so each partner can combine their tastes. It's the way the traditional trade can get back.'

In any case, James is optimistic about the competition. 'I think the supermarkets have peaked. To me they are an extension of the Blue Nun and Mateus Rosé syndrome. I think they do a lot for the wine trade in general. Although they're not into the fine wine market, they've got more people to drink wine because it's part of their daily shopping. But the taste has to be fairly innocuous because otherwise they will upset people. Drinking for experience and drinking value for money are different. Under the £3 mark people don't experiment much.'

Rogers was evidently confident in 1984 that Cullens would continue to expand, selling to wine enthusiasts who had progressed from the mass market. Indeed they may expand, but it is curious to me that they continue to play down their origins as grocers. It seems as mistaken, in its way, as Fortnum & Mason's evident determination to turn themselves into a department store. For there is clearly a need for a new type of emporium: the wine warehouse that sells top-quality food, together with cookery equipment, glasses, books on food and wine and everything else for the gourmet who appreciates the range offered by the supermarkets but wants better quality and personal service.

James Rogers is a horse-racing enthusiast but he continues to bet each way on three or four nags rather than placing his shirt to win on the outside chance.

That, at least, was my conclusion. But I had overlooked the traditional pattern of these things; the fact that there is always a bidder in the wings, waiting like the *deus ex machina* of seventeenth-century masques to shower gold and good fortune on the poor entangled mortals. In the masque, that was the end of the business, as the curtain dropped amid general rejoicing. In reality the new owners of Cullens have their work cut out, writing the script for the next act.

Sainsbury's: Allan Cheesman

I was interviewing my editor when Allan Cheesman rang from Sainsbury's to confirm a meeting. After he and Jancis had made their arrangements I took the telephone and asked for his views on the future of the wine trade.

He replied with uncharacteristic caution, realizing this was on the record. There was a pause, then a laugh and then the cocky cry of the boy waving his wooden sword on the top of the sandhill. 'Adnams and Tanners put on yer tin 'ats!'

He has a right to his triumph for he has risen, purely by merit, to one of the most influential positions in the English wine trade, buying for a company that's surging ahead at a formidable rate. He has the jaunty air of the man who sells one in every seven bottles of wine consumed in Britain.

Backing this confidence is the knowledge that the supermarkets have come from a standing start to control 54 per cent of the retail wine business, and the belief that wine consumption in Britain will treble in the next ten to fifteen years. But it's a fiercely competitive world. As Allan looks over the weekly price check of leading lines in the other supermarket groups, he shakes his head in disbelief: 'Some of these boys can't work out the VAT!'

The closest Allan got to a wine trade background was the fact that his parents retired to run a pub in Surrey, but his ambition was clear from an early age – he wanted to join the Navy. Turned down at the last minute because of his eyesight (a bitter blow), he went into banking but got bored and looked around for something else.

On 1 June 1971 (Allan has a mania for dates) he joined Sainsbury's as a 'management trainee in productivity services' (work study) at the age of twenty-one. During the course of the next year his work gave him a useful overall grasp of the workings of the company, and he kept his eyes on the notice boards (it's Sainsbury's policy to advertise all jobs internally). In July 1972 he applied for the post of trainee wine buyer and was taken on in the off-licence department, which at that time totalled five people 'including the man who went out and got the licences'. Seventy-five branches had a licence (there are 250 now) and 'we were growing. . . . We were just starting to motor on original bottling, with Sainsbury's name on the label.'

Andrew Nunn was table wine buyer. 'He had a very good palate, and taught me a lot but he was very much in the wine trade mould. He looked on Sainsbury's as a wine merchant selling groceries, but of course it's the reverse; we're a supermarket selling wine.

'The senior manager was Ron Perry, an old Sainsbury's hand. He was a brilliant negotiator, never said a word. The supplier talked himself into a lower price just to fill the silence.'

There's certainly no silence to fill with Allan Cheesman – he must browbeat his suppliers with words; fluent, articulate, enthusiastic and irresistible.

'I was buying all the odds and ends then – the cartons, corks, bottles etc. There were safraps of Moroccan red arriving to be bottled. It was fierce stuff (one customer complained because his tongue went black) but it sold for 38 pence a bottle in 1972. Duty was £1.6125 per gallon, and the cost of the wine itself was only 20 pence per gallon, delivered!'

It is typical of Allan to remember all the percentage points. And the dates. 'September 1st 1973, the date that we joined the Common Market and became subject to EEC wine laws, that was a milestone, critical for the trade.' Indeed it was. The acceptance by Britain of the appellation laws finished off a traditional market in spurious burgundy and other wines (coming at the same time as the collapse of the fine wine boom, it also finished off some traditional merchants) and the enforcement of the appellation not only gave the consumer greater confidence in what he was buying, but accelerated the move towards bottling at source.

Alan took the various wine trade examinations, passing the Diploma (with Honours) in 1975 and winning himself a scholarship. He was becoming a specialist, something atypical in the Sainsbury's system where buyers tend to be a generic breed, switching readily from frozen food to fresh vegetables to washing-powder. In 1975 Andrew Nunn moved on and Allan became buyer of table and fortified wines, responsible for between twenty and thirty products in Sainsbury's 'own-label' range.

'In 1978, when Ron Perry retired, I was promoted to senior manager, head of one of the twenty-three buying offices of Sainsbury's. I had two or three buyers working for me and I reported direct to Bob Ingham, one of the main board directors.'

Allan Cheesman was just twenty-eight.

'1978 was the big springboard for the company. We launched a big discount campaign and had a real surge. Things were motoring. We were beginning to expand into Italy and the number of our own-label wines was growing. In the space of two years we added thirty-seven wines with our own label (all but three bottled in the country of origin). I worked closely with our design department. We developed the back label and so on. We spent a lot of money creating the Sainsbury's brand; advertising, PR, design work etc.

'On 5th January 1980 they decided to give me the whole lot. I got beers and spirits as well. You have a totally different sort of buying operation, different sorts of people – the big brewers, brand-owners etc. It was fascinating, a challenge, coming into contact with that side of the business.'

Some people are loners. Cheesman, by contrast, is the best type of large company employee; able to retain his enthusiasm and individuality while working through the complex systems of a big organization.

'I've been at the helm at a very exciting time – not just for wine but for Sainsbury's. I've had the backing, resources and development of a very successful company. It's alchemy.

'We are not just buyers but product managers. We have a design input on the product, right from the beginning. We are responsible from the vine (or at least the bottling-line) to the dinner table or from the brewhouse to the pint mug. There are all sorts of aspects to the job, involving other people in the company – the marketing boys, the design department and so on. We come up with the ideas but other people translate them into practice.'

There is undeniably a 'supermarket style' that results from this approach, and it is interesting to note that the buyers for Tesco, Asda and International Stores are all ex-Sainsbury men, something of which Allan Cheesman is proud and a little concerned too! 'We seem to have taken over from Harveys of Bristol as the wine trade training ground.'

Not everyone shares his enthusiasm at this piece of news, for a good many wine lovers see the supermarket 'own-label' range as offering the dull decency of wines blended for general acceptability: good value but characterless. The same can be said of the big advertised brands sold by the brewery-owned off-licences but everyone expects dreariness of the brewers, who have come closer than anyone to destroying the quality of life for the English drinker. Better things are expected of the supermarkets.

And, in fact, better things are coming. Champagne (a wine that has to be blended if it is going to be any good) was added to the 'own-label' range and then Sainsbury's woke up to the fact that Waitrose (supermarket offshoot of the John Lewis Partnership) had proved that there *was* an alternative to shelves full of Liebfraumilch and Anjou Rosé. Waitrose won themselves critical acclaim from the wine journalists by an imaginative selection of characterful, individual wines from named vineyards. Sainsbury's, following their example, did likewise.

'Our Vintage Selection started because we had carved out a pretty big niche for our own-label wines and we felt there was room for trading up. We were losing customers to the specialists who had the top wines in their range. But rather than just having the château label we had to identify it as Sainsbury's. So we came up with the idea, and then investigated how we should do it and the answer was Vintage Selection, with the seal on the label, carrying our name. And it works – we now have people coming to us asking if we will include their wines in the range. We've got things like Château Cissac 1973, Perriet Jouet 1978, Viña Ardanza 1976, Villa Antinori 1979, Torres Gran Coronas 1978, Grahams Malvedos 1968 Vintage Port. We have amazing flexibility. We can handle hundreds of thousands of cases of Liebfraumilch or a few cases of Corton Grancey from Louis Latour which we'll put into our prestige wine branch in the Cromwell Road.'

The wines are no longer chosen solely from samples submitted by middlemen. An increasing proportion is bought direct ex-cellar, *clos* or château. In the meantime, the quality and the flexibility that Allan mentions are formidable additional weapons in the fight for market share.

'The supermarket area now has 54 per cent of the total wine trade. I can see it consolidating. We are opening fifteen shops a year for the foreseeable future, and we're moving north in quite a way; a

Savacentre hypermarket (a joint venture between Sainsbury's and British Home Stores) has just opened in Edinburgh. So our volume will continue to increase, but I don't see the supermarkets' share rising much above 60 per cent because the off-licences are fighting back (look at the Victoria Wine approach) and so are the real specialists, people like Adnams and Tanners; you've got a countryside reputation. Yapps do good business from a very small base, Cullens innovate all the time and Lay & Wheeler extend their range.

'Of course, we've taken trade from the brewery off-licences but we've also grown the business. We've popularized wine but left some mystique in it. We've pioneered clear, concise labelling and we've published our own wine books by people such as Hugh Johnson and Christopher Fielden.'

Indeed, whatever reservations you have about the quality of some of the basic supermarket wines it is undeniable that Sainsbury's has been in the lead in making wine easy and familiar to a completely new public.

'We site our off-licences at one side of the exit end of the branches so that people can browse. We recognize that it is the female who is making the alcohol purchase decision – 80 per cent of our customers are women.'

And the supermarkets have been successful in promoting a clean, modern image, neutral in terms of class or sex – something that is emphatically not true of most off-licence chains. So it is hardly surprising that the brewers got worried.

'The off-licences haven't got the customer throughput (we serve up to 6 million people a week) and they haven't got the locations – there's no car parking outside them. But the brewers have got a lot of money and the future will be very interesting.'

Whatever the outcome of this war, Allan Cheesman has enormous confidence in the future of his trade. 'Wine has what I call the three "V's". It has value; we have forty-nine wines on our shelves under £2 per bottle [as at November 1984]. It has variety; there are thousands of different wines from all over the world and they've all got a bit of magic, a story, a special sound. And it has versatility; you can enjoy wine any time of day you like, in any circumstances, from Buck's Fizz at breakfast, to a glass at a party in the middle of the night. It's my hobby-horse, it really is. In Britain we're drinking around ten litres per head at present. I reckon we'll double consumption by the end of the decade and add another ten litres by 1995.

'We have to be careful. We do have a social responsibility if we're selling liquor in terms of the training of staff, control of sales etc. I'm well aware of it and the subject is always on the agenda at committee meetings of the British Retailers Group, on which I sit.'

What will we be drinking and how will it be packed? The traditionalist surfaces.

'I still like the bottle with a cork in it. I was pushed into wine boxes. Happily they are levelling off as a percentage of our trade. It's convenient. But it's a dangerous way of consuming wine because you can't see the level going down. Also I do get concerned about the quality. There are still a lot of keeping problems to which we don't know all the answers.

'But you can't ignore alternative methods of packaging – tetra-bricks, cans and so on. All of these things have been very successful in bringing a new public to enjoy wine.

'There is a shortage of quality wine for specific markets – you try and buy Chablis or Beaujolais now. It will be interesting when Spain and Portugal join the Common Market and I haven't written off California. Of course now that the exchange rate is so low, it's nothing like as attractive as when we started buying at $2.46 but I am convinced it will be an important supplier to the European market in the twenty-first century.

'I love France. I'm a dedicated Francophile and I'm sure we'll continue to see that as the source of quality. Italy will be more important, but the trouble with the Italian wine market is that it was founded on the Italian restaurant business and the versatility of Italian wine is not as great as others. But the consistency is now much better and there are some fine wines coming out. Spain I see as being a couple of years behind Italy, with a lot of wonderful wines waiting to be discovered.

'It comes back to versatility and variety. There are so many wines and I can enjoy wine in any circumstances, whether it's one of those that we sell for less than £2 or a great bottle of claret. It's horses for courses.

'The danger for the supplying companies is that soon there will only be a dozen major buying points and the competition to get listed will be terrific.'

That seemed to me rather a bleak view of the future, implying the disappearance of the independent merchants. Did Allan really see us having such a hard time, sitting in the trenches with our tin hats on?

He laughed. 'If you project present trends you realize that Sainsbury's will be the only supermarket group in Britain by 1993 and in Europe by 2012. We all know that's not going to happen. . . . Providing you at Adnams can offer a service you will survive and you won't need to wear a helmet. But you'd better lay in a bit of extra food and ammunition!'

XII
The Auctioneers

The Rivals

'Sotheby's are auctioneers trying to be gents, while Christie's are gentlemen trying to be auctioneers.'

The much-repeated catchphrase infuriates members of both these great London auction houses but, like most such tags, it does contain an element of truth. The siting of their premises is indicative. Sotheby's is in busy Bond Street, home of the deluxe emporia frequented by wealthy foreigners. The kerbs are crawling with rich riffraff. Christie's is in the quieter backwater of King Street, St James's, halfway between Fortnum & Mason and the grand gentlemen's clubs of Pall Mall. The rivalry is intense and these internationally famous firms maintain their distinct identities. They do join together somewhat infrequently for mainly charitable causes but, between times, they compete furiously for business and for publicity.

In fact, the only time when they appeared to have adopted a common front was when they simultaneously introduced the buyer's premium on the sales of works of art. It was a move that managed to alienate all their major clients (the dealers), and gained a considerable amount of adverse publicity.

Traditionally, the English auctioneers had made their living from the commission charged to the seller, normally between 10 and 15 per cent. The addition of a further 10 per cent margin at the expense of the buyer not only enabled the auction houses to provide the increasingly expensive expert services demanded by their clients, but also gave them the opportunity to compete on cutthroat terms for the very best sales. Secure in their fixed percentage from the buyer, they could slash the vendor's commission to nothing at all in order to get their hands on the most valuable collections. It was the London dealers who bore the brunt of this new imposition and they squealed loudly. Legal proceedings were instigated (charging Christie's and Sotheby's with collusion) and after a good deal of public argument there was an out-of-court settlement that did little to change the new rules. Christie's reduced their buyer's premium to 8 per cent.*

Neither house, however, charged a premium on wine. Recognizing that this particular commodity market was already sufficiently complicated by duty and VAT, and fearing that a further percentage might lead to significantly lower prices, the auctioneers decided to except their Wine Departments from the general rule. This tacit understanding was broken in the summer of 1984 when Sotheby's suddenly and unilaterally extended the premium to wine sales. The result was an unexpected 'breaking of ranks' as Christie's engaged in forthright public criticism of their competitor, and the battle between the Wine Departments became the focus of the bitterest expressions of the ill-will that subsisted between the two great auction houses.

The dispute was twenty years in the making. Christie's was the first of the auctioneers to realize that the increasing interest in classic wine (on both sides of the Atlantic) could form the basis of a new market, and that they could offer an important service to their traditional clients by helping them dispose of valuable family cellars, accumulated over several generations. They started their Wine Department in 1966 and Sotheby's followed suit in 1970. But Christie's were able to build on a commanding lead.

They began with the announcement that they were resuming wine sales (they had indeed sold wine regularly over the previous two hundred years), and this claim was reinforced by the acquisition in 1966 of the century-old City wine auctioneers, W. & T. Restell. To be sure, Christie's had not sold wine for over twenty years and Restell's monthly sales were drab affairs, consisting mostly of 'bin-ends' of trade stock, but both firms had tremendous aristocratic connections (source of many wonderful cellars for future sales) and, equally important, the merger brought together two very different characters in an often uncomfortable, but highly productive, partnership.

* Increases to 10 per cent with effect from September 1986.

Michael Broadbent had applied to Christie's when he heard they were thinking of starting a Wine Department. He got the job because he wanted it badly enough, had all the necessary talents and was backed by a tremendously good reference from his former boss at Harveys of Bristol, Harry Waugh. Not only was he already an expert taster, good organizer, experienced lecturer and writer on wine, but his face fitted. Though actually the son of a Yorkshire mill-owning family, Michael had always *looked* like a director of Christie's: tall, distinguished, elegantly clad, undoubtedly a gentleman. But appearances are deceptive. Behind the witty, well-mannered but rather austere façade lurks a man who is livelier, funnier, sharper and more combative than you would expect; an amusing, sometimes malicious gossip who can be ruthlessly quick on the draw.

One of Broadbent's most attractive characteristics is his evident ability to command the affection of his staff. To this generalization, however, there is apparently one exception: his most valuable assistant!

Alan Taylor-Restell had for years acted as dogsbody to an authoritative father, the sole partner and owner of W. & T. Restell. Tom Restell was known in the City as 'the Vicar', partly because he looked like one and partly, according to Robin Kernick of Corney & Barrow, 'because he would rechristen any wine at the drop of a hat!' When the old man had a heart attack in early 1966 Alan found himself, at the age of twenty-seven, master of a business that was running rapidly downhill. Unable to raise any capital from the banks, he was forced to seek a merger at about the time that Christie's announced they were going to restart wine sales. 'My stepfather was an antique dealer, very friendly with Arthur Grimwade, the silver expert here. Through him an approach was made to see if there might be a chance of joining forces.' It was a marriage of convenience. 'If it works it works. Personally, deep down, I'm a man who would have preferred to remain independent. The choice was not mine.'

Nonetheless, there were considerable advantages for both sides. In Michael's words, 'He brought with him the solid technical background of a third-generation City wine auctioneer, and left me free to develop hitherto parochial sales into the present international operation.' But it remains a partnership of contrasts, of near incompatible personalities, as both sides openly admit. Where Michael is urbane, self-confident and well organized (his tasting records are the wonder of the wine trade), Alan (rounder, shorter, with a domed, bespectacled head) is rumpled, easily upset and bad at delegating. He is, however, extremely good at his job.

In conversation with Michael Broadbent I have the impression that he believes he is a better auctioneer than Alan. That may be true when Michael is in action at really spectacular events, like the show-piece auctions in America when his self-confidence and sense of occasion are unmatched, but for the rest it is Alan who has the edge in the opinion of most regular buyers and of Christie's rivals in Bond Street. Pat Grubb (ex-Sotheby's) is quick to acknowledge it. 'I think Alan's probably the best wine auctioneer there is. He has a wonderful memory for names and he is *extremely* quick which is very important in wine sales because there's nothing visual and the speed tends to hurry people into making a decision.'

After nearly twenty years working together, Broadbent and Restell still fight it out every day. Alan is working at his desk when Michael pops in, looking preoccupied. 'I've got Dr F. from Paris in my office. I must let him know what's happening about that magnum of '53 Pétrus that got stolen.' Alan looks blank. 'Do you remember? When I checked the case at Trapp's cellars there were only two magnums, not three.' Alan assumes the face of an injured dogsbody. 'I was told to have nothing to do with wines shipped over from France, to keep my nose out of it. So I've not dealt with any of these shipments. I haven't the foggiest idea!'

Michael, rather cross: 'Who told you that?'

Alan, enjoying the moment: 'You did! You'd better ask Duncan about it. If you or he haven't made a claim on the shipping company then presumably nothing's been done.'

Such dogfights should not mislead the unwary. This is a formidable team with unmatchable experience.

They started with spectacular successes, like the huge trade disposal from Alexis Lichine and a series of sales of great family cellars that began with the astounding collection of ancient bottles from Lord Rosebery. This particular sale really rankled in Bond Street. 'Sotheby's had already sold an attic full of £2 million worth of furniture for Rosebery and then Christie's got his wine!' But the crunch came in 1970 when Christie's sold the cellars of Glamis Castle, property of the Bowes Lyon family, royal cousins and long-time Sotheby clients. There was even a Bowes Lyon on the Sotheby board! They realized that they were in danger of losing long-standing clients to

Christie's if they did not offer a comparable service and so started their own Wine Department in 1970.

But Sotheby's were late in the field and chose the wrong man. Colin Fenton may have seemed a Broadbent lookalike (Master of Wine, ex-Harveys of Bristol, elegant, urbane) but he did not have the same strength of character, imagination or attention to detail. He was so shy that he proved unable to conduct his own wine sales which had to be taken for him by auctioneers from other departments of the firm. They held only eight wine sales a year and the wine business was rightly regarded as the poor relation of the company by the other directors at Sotheby's.

In 1973 Fenton was replaced by Patrick Grubb, a director of Lebègue, well-respected London shippers renowned for their vast annual tastings for the trade. Pat is quiet, decent and competent, but his virtues are those of the traditional wine trade (to which he has now returned); not the showman. Nonetheless, he took his own sales and developed provincial auctions throughout the country and overseas sales in Holland and Switzerland. He was the first to publish estimates alongside the lots in the catalogues but the drab green covers of these publications were never as enticing as the lively claret red of Christie's. Hamstrung by long-standing deficiencies of organization and reputation, Sotheby's Wine Department continued to resemble a poor reflection of its glamorous rival, and Pat Grubb himself acquired a periodic air of melancholy.

So matters proceeded through periods of boom, slump and renewed boom with Christie's being highly successful and Sotheby's tagging along in their wake. Michael Broadbent started a wine publications department and wrote books and wine articles, proving himself a master of publicity. Having organized the first big Heublein sale in the States in 1969, he then helped start the even more remarkable Napa Valley wine auctions, as well as running a few Christie's sales in Chicago and elsewhere. Pat Grubb comments sadly that: 'We did one auction of our own in America, but our office there didn't help very much and Michael had been scooping the ground away very successfully.' He was invited to be guest auctioneer at the annual Nederburg wine auction in South Africa and has pioneered wine sales in Japan. All of these highly publicized overseas affairs brought foreign buyers to both houses, but it was the American market that was to prove of critical importance, and there Christie's dominance is unquestionable.

Wine sales at the best of times represented a relatively small part of each auctioneer's turnover, which remained dominated by jewels, furniture and fine art. Both houses expanded their activities in these areas by substantial investment overseas, particularly in the States, while Sotheby's spent heavily on property. The property boom collapsed in 1973, as did many other speculative markets (including wine) and the great auctioneers suffered major reverses. Sotheby's was worst hit and, having turned itself into a public company, was vulnerable to predators.

Along came the sharks. Armed with the profits of their American office furniture business, Messrs Cogan and Swid started buying up Sotheby's shares. They sounded like villains, and that is certainly how they were seen by their intended prey. There was a drawn-out, bitter battle for ownership that focused public attention on Sotheby's troubles, particularly after hysterical statements were made by one or two hard-pressed senior directors. In the event, Sotheby's only succeeded in fighting off one American takeover by soliciting another. Alfred A. Taubmann, a multi-millionaire from Michigan, rode to the rescue in the nick of time, bought out Cogan and Swid and everyone else, gave all the staff a pay rise and demanded, not unreasonably, greater attention to the bottom line.

Two small departments (Coins and Medals, and Wine) were increasingly under pressure on this score. Neither charged the buyer's premium and the Wine Department had hardly made money since its inception (unlike their rivals at Christie's). The annual turnover of each section was easily exceeded by a single successful sale of gems or paintings. The Coins and Medals Department was the first to crack, and introduced the buyer's premium at the beginning of 1984. The much-feared effect on prices (in a commodity market of repeatable items) failed to materialize and one of the main arguments of the opponents of the premium was quashed. The Wine Department could not hold out much longer. 'We'd been talking about ways and means of improving our service, but to pay for the improvements we had to introduce the premium.' Patrick Grubb was determined to extricate his Department from an intolerable situation. 'I felt very strongly that we were not accepted because we were a loss-maker, and I was damned if we should go on being subsidized by other departments.'

Both Bonham's and Phillips had packed up *their* wine auctions. finding themselves unable to generate sufficient profit, and Grubb must have feared the same fate. He recognized that the extra 10 per cent on the hammer price would probably hit their sales of price-sensitive 'bin-ends' (not-so-new-Beaujolais Nouveau and the like), but he wasn't worried about losing this business. 'We were spending so much time and effort handling this very basic trade stuff at absolutely no profit, and the merchants were always complaining about us taking business from them. So I thought let's get rid of that side of it.' The fine wine market was booming, thanks largely to the strength of the dollar, and Patrick calculated that he could retain his share of this trade and, at last, make money.

Sotheby's introduced the premium without warning, mid-season, shortly before what had been billed as their best-ever wine sale. There is no denying that the timing was clumsy and that Pat Grubb devoted insufficient attention to public relations, in striking contrast to his opposite number in King Street.

Michael Broadbent had a field day. Where Grubb initially contented himself with a bald announcement of the premium and of new, more competitive commission rates to the vendor, Broadbent (never slow to take the offensive) launched broadside after broadside at his foe. But the very speed and vigour of his reaction may have led him to overstate his position in terms that will prove embarrassing if Christie's is ever forced to follow Sotheby's lead. In letters to his clients and the trade press he restated his opposition to the premium, avowed that it would not be introduced at Christie's and spoke with disdain of the success and expertise of his rivals. Confident of his commanding lead he wrote: 'We know, because our clients tell us, that our long-experienced team is far and away the most efficient in this highly specialized business.' In a sale memorandum he included a 'History of Wine Auctions – Sotheby's please note' and he went on to refer to their 'extravagant claims and misleading statements. . . . Pure propaganda'. Broadbent accused his rivals of being 'an *extremely* aggressive firm' but his language was certainly inflamed by the heat of battle and in conversation he was even more caustic than in print.

The claims and counter-claims about prices and estimates became increasingly technical, and it was hard to draw any firm conclusions from the tail-end sales that completed the summer season of 1984. Nonetheless, Pat Grubb seemed to be losing the publicity war, even if his reticence lent him a certain dignity. He has, in any case, naturally melancholy eyes and it is hard not to feel sympathy for him. He occasionally gets patronized by *sommeliers*, something that never happens to Broadbent ('very nice, very sweet' says the waiter at the Oriental Club as he serves 1959 Moulin Touchais with the pudding). And by late 1984 he was clearly unhappy in his job.'I do tend to feel that one's on a treadmill, getting clients together, the catalogues, the publicity etc. It can become a very boring business and though there are lots of benefits it's a very unrelaxing job. But one of the things I've enjoyed very much is the people in the Department. They are a very good team.'

But the team had not managed to achieve the reputation for efficient service that was increasingly expected, and their promises to do better with the premium did seem limp. In any case, as Alan Taylor-Restell pointed out, expectations would be raised. 'People who pay the premium are going to demand premium service. But you can't be perfect with a third party to deal with. You can't get goods out of bond in an hour.'

The issue was unresolved as the auctioneers packed up for the summer recess (a habit they share with politicians and academics). Then in the dead time of mid-August another circular arrived from Sotheby's, announcing free delivery, free insurance, free wine-finding facilities and free handling of all export documentation. 'If I was a big buyer I'd ask for a collection allowance,' commented Broadbent, but the stakes were clearly raised and Grubb redoubled the attack in a letter that appeared in the August issue of *Decanter* magazine. Most of the arguments had already been aired but he finished on a fighting note: 'Our sales' content and catalogues are already of infinitely better quality than those of our rivals!'

This was clearly tongue-in-cheek and for a moment the debate lightened as Broadbent responded in a similar mood: 'I concede that the cover of the Sotheby's 6-7 June catalogue was most attractive; an excellent (and costly) example of the art of the photographer and the skill of the printer. Maybe his buyers are happy for part of their extra 10 per cent to be devoted to the glamorization of what is essentially a piece of ephemera? The Bible had a phrase for this: "a whited sepulchre"!'

He continued, however, with an admirably clear résumé of the problem that now confronted Christie's. 'The real catch in the current situation is that, in order to entice business, Sotheby's vendors' commission can be reduced literally to nil, the auctioneer taking comfort in the knowledge that he will at least have the 10 per cent buyer's premium in his coffers. . . . If we are ever forced to follow suit, it will be . . . because of Sotheby's cutting to shreds their vendors' commission to boost turnover.'

Arguably, as I write, it is indeed only a matter of time before Christie's is forced to follow its rival's example.* Despite his remarks about 'whited sepulchres' Broadbent's immediate reaction was to upgrade the appearance of his own catalogues. Every such move is another bite out of Wine Department profits. It may be hard to maintain Christie's commanding lead without having the additional commission income to justify expensive improvements in service and presentation. Nonetheless, Broadbent remained confident while Pat Grubb decided that he personally had had enough: as the autumn season drew to a close he announced that he was leaving Sotheby's to start a new wine company. His deputy, David Molyneux-Berry, was left in charge to continue the fight with Christie's.

Whatever the outcome of this particular battle, the noisy arguments will soon seem of minor consequence. More important issues will come to the fore, notably the long-standing debate over whether the great auction houses should take a hand in the *primeur* market, selling the new vintages of the great Bordeaux châteaux (Christie's are against the idea, Sotheby's tentatively in favour).

But the fight over the premium, unimportant in itself, did reveal the highly aggressive instincts that lay behind the urbane good manners of the participants, a ferocity that is extremely rare in the wine trade. The 'breaking of ranks' is probably permanent, whether or not Pat Grubb's successor outmanoeuvres his flamboyant rival, and the bitterness will linger. Talking of auctioneers and gentlemen is anachronistic. They are all professionals.

Finest and Rarest

'The learned bubble of the saleroom and varnishing auctioneer.'

Thomas Carlyle: *Frederick the Great*

There is a seediness about auction rooms, a tawdry, second-hand shabbiness which is reflected in a good many of the habitués. Even the greatest masterpieces seem, for a moment, second-rate in such

---

* A prophecy fulfilled. In June 1986 Christie's Wine Department announced that they were introducing a Buyer's Premium with effect from the following September.

surroundings. But there is also a glamour beneath the grime, the excitement that attaches to big names and big money, to transatlantic bidding by telephone and the flickering board that translates the ever-mounting price into the leading currencies of the world. The auctioneers know how to intensify this sense of occasion, of theatre. A quip lightens the atmosphere or encourages the hesitant buyer, and then the voice becomes quieter, seemingly casual as a duel develops for possession of an especially desirable lot. Attention is focused on the raised finger at the back of the room or the almost imperceptible nod at the front. It is like gambling when the bets are doubled. The bidders find themselves the focus of tension, engaged in a public battle in which their courage as much as their money is at stake. But it is a fragile thing and the slightest shock or error on the part of the auctioneer can awaken the protagonists to the enormity of the sums involved. As in fishing, the gentlest touch can land a plump buyer who would otherwise take fright if a sudden jerk distracted his attention from the brilliant lure to the line that trailed it or the hand that reeled it in.

It would be easy to imagine that the experienced dealers and wealthy collectors never subject themselves to the thrills and terrors of the amateur, that they are never trapped by the compulsive madness that seizes the occasional buyer who awakens to find that he has spent more than he intended or could afford. But in fact the whole business depends on the continuing willingness of the professionals to overstep, by however modest a margin, the furthest limit they had set for themselves. It is like the game of grandmother's footsteps.

On a sunny morning in June the sale rooms in King Street were crowded with dealers, viewing the furniture that was to be sold on the following day (rather grand stuff, set out in a tremendous clutter below numerous large and mostly bad pictures), and with all manner of people who had come to look at the Chatsworth drawings. The Duke of Devonshire, perennially short of cash, had decided to clear out a few 'seconds' from his vast collection: three or four marvellous sketches by Rembrandt; a watercolour landscape by Van Dyck; one superb and two doubtful drawings by Raphael; some caricatures ascribed to Leonardo and a number of fine works by lesser masters. A few days later the Duke was richer by over £20 million and Christie's had garnered a handsome commission.

An ante-room had cases stacked with fine porcelain, and in another corner they were sorting out some rather dreary Japanese screens. In the midst of this intriguing mixture of unrelated objects (rather like a very grand junk shop) was a small area, corralled off from the hurly-burly by showcases that normally held minor valuables and were now filled with old bottles and corkscrews. In the middle of this 'pen' was a table on which were laid out four or five bottles of old port, a few clarets and two or three burgundies – samples of the rarities that were to be auctioned in Christie's wine sale on the morrow. A couple of prospective buyers were tasting the wines with Alan Taylor-Restell, immune to the surrounding bustle. Michael Broadbent arrived and began making notes in his neat and methodical way, muttering 'varnishy' when he came to the 1908 Offley, but showing justified enthusiasm for the Cockburn 1912, a wonderful, soft and velvety port with an elegant, pot-pourri complexity of bouquet.

I noticed a bottle of 1946 Mouton Rothschild in the showcase, a poor vintage (the year of my birth), and was startled to see the estimate set at over £1,000 for the single bottle. 'The wine's actually not bad, but it's the label they're after. It's a great rarity, the first of the pictorial labels from Mouton, and there are collectors who must have the full set.' I pointed out that it was rather faded and slightly torn, though described as 'perfect' in the catalogue. 'It must have happened when they were unpacking it,' said Broadbent. 'We'll have to announce it from the rostrum.' An assistant offered to glue the tear back in place.

In the Wine Department offices there were constant interruptions as everyone prepared for the next day's sale. Telephone calls from clients leaving commissions to bid or getting information about interesting lots were interspersed with enquiries from the Press or the arrival of a hopeful vendor with a couple of unusual bottles. With a preoccupied and slightly flustered air, Alan Taylor-Restell was copying reserves and commissions into his copy of the catalogue while Michael dealt with an elderly American general from Kentucky, a wine enthusiast who had, it seemed, simply dropped in for a chat. The general reminisced with no thought for the business of the day but in a pungent entertaining style that excused his haphazard ramblings.

'You remember that little do we had on Concorde for the Chianti Classico at Christie's? That Beychevelle '24. . . . What a party! That very attractive lady I was with, she was rather . . . well-endowed. We were in Italy in some palace outside Florence. We each presented ourselves in front of this councillor and he knighted each of the *Legata del Chianti* with this vine root. He touched, I guess, her left shoulder and then raised the root and gazed down at her bosom and missed her right shoulder altogether. "Hey," I said. "You spoiled the ceremony!"' The old boy rattled on while Michael poured the champagne and, at a table in the background, Pat Matthews and Christopher Bradshaw worked, quite unperturbed, on the layout of the latest of the Christie's wine publications, a lengthy book on Madeira by Noël Cossart.

Eventually the general decided to go. 'This is what occupies my days,' said Michael. 'I work between five and seven . . . then at home after dinner and every weekend!'

He showed me round. It was all very labour-intensive. The single computer screen is hidden in the small office where the cataloguing is done by Digby Lang, who has the air of a Dickensian clerk and works from piles of laboriously hand-written cards. 'Still the most flexible and effective way,' insists Broadbent, who has clearly never worked with a word processor. 'Every detail counts – we get it wrong and it costs us money.' He stresses that 'Catalogues are more important than auctioneers – the skill lies in correctly judged lot sizes, arrangement and general credibility.'

Where does the constant stream of fine wine come from? 'There's quite a lot of trade stock and the top London merchants [Berry Bros, Justerini's, Corney & Barrow] regularly send clients round here to sell their private cellars. But the great undiscovered cellars are in France, not in England any more. The trouble about dealing with the French is that they expect ridiculously high prices.

'I usually refuse to have stuff back for resale from America. There's the problem of condition. The buyer can always ask the provenance and if the wine comes from trade stock it is sampled. Below a certain condition it is sent to South Kensington or offered subject to sample.'

Provenance and condition are, indeed, the biggest problems about buying at auction, given the way fine wine deteriorates if it is moved too often or badly stored. Old wine can be wonderful, but sometimes old wine has been traded too frequently and is long past its best. Overheated restaurant stock is not recommended.

'About 90 per cent of what we sell is Bordeaux, and roughly 60 per cent of that is sold to overseas customers of whom 60 per cent are Americans. The market's very strong at the moment because of the strength of the dollar but claret will go down if the dollar sinks. We used to have a lot of small private buyers but now we have a few very rich ones. It's not unusual for someone to fly in for a sale and spend £30,000.'

We went to lunch. The *sommelier* at the Stafford produced a bottle of New York State wine on which he wanted Broadbent's opinion. 'Rusty nails,' was the comment of the man whose book on wine-tasting has sold 160,000 copies throughout the world.

The day of the sale. 'Finest and Rarest Wines and Collectors' Pieces', announces the catalogue ambivalently. Buyers have arrived from Europe and America and the room is moderately full when Alan Taylor-Restell mounts the rostrum promptly at eleven o'clock.

'There is no buyer's premium at this sale,' he says, looking hard at the representative from Sotheby's who has come to observe the proceedings, and then he sets off at the rattling pace for which he is famous.

'I wasn't made with the gift of the gab. I am a very nervous and quiet character but I can get myself worked up for an auction. I can turn myself on and make the sale fire. You can have a beautiful catalogue but you bloody well need an auctioneer to get it going.' Alan's opinion is shared by his rival, Pat Grubb. 'When it's a slightly unusual auction the auctioneer is very important. He has to draw people out of themselves. It's a cross between being a preacher and an actor.'

Alan is certainly drawing out his audience to great effect today. Helped by the strong dollar, prices are soaring, and in the first few minutes of the sale a case of 1945 Mouton (estimate over £3,000) goes for £5,300, to an American bidder.

At a high desk below the rostrum Odette Ryan, the cashier, sits beside a newly recruited member of staff, noting down prices and buyers' names and sorting through the blue 'commission to bid' forms that are brought from the office as the last minute bidders come through on the telephone. Nearby sit Duncan McEuen, the director responsible for the Geneva and Amsterdam sales, and Michael Broadbent, the boss. They are busy scribbling the prices in their catalogues and scanning the audience to note who is bidding.

It is a motley gathering, reminiscent of a cartoon by Rowlandson or Hogarth. The London dealers, friendly rivals, tend to cluster at the back of the room, murmuring and smiling as they compete for the various lots. One of them is a specialist in recorked wines for the American market and he bids high for ullaged bottles. 'We're happy to have a gang of trade dealers who will sell on in the States,' says Broadbent. 'The Americans are so much trouble to deal with.'

At the front of the room sits Edmund Penning-Rowsell, wine correspondent of the *Financial Times* and author of the classic work on Bordeaux. He is carefully noting the prices for an article in one of the trade magazines. Just behind him, also scribbling in his catalogue, is a very strange fish; pale, paunchy, in a dusty black three-piece suit, he holds the catalogue an inch from his face, screwing up his eyes to read the words as his thick pebble glasses rest on his knee. He rarely bids but smiles wryly from time to time as he jots down the price of every lot. A couple of rows back two men with grey, unhealthy, night-owl faces look half asleep in creased jeans and uncombed hair. One of them is the brother of a film star and bids occasionally for old port and Auslese Moselle. Beside him is a small elderly man with a crumpled face in a rumpled suit and cardigan, typecast as an old-fashioned corner grocer. And near the back, a trio of late arrivals excites attention. She is a sleepy, sexy Jeanne Moreau lookalike and he is a blank-faced, pin-striped smoothie; their friend is dressed as a gangster, in dark glasses and a sharp, cream suit.

A battle develops for the 1899 Pichon Longueville. Alan's voice lowers to a conspiratorial murmur as his head moves like a bird's, tick-tack, tick-tack, from one protagonist to the other. 'You can't afford to have a monotonous voice,' explains Alan. 'People fall asleep. You can't predict how it will go but if you're lucky you get a laugh and a gasp of "What an incredible price!"' It happens now as one of the dealers pays well over the odds for badly ullaged bottles of very old wine. It was a good demonstration of Alan's technique. 'If you stare at somebody long enough you'll push them one step too far. If you swing onto them quickly enough you've made the decision for them and they nod and accept it. But it does *not* pay to drag it out to the last pound. People start chatting behind your back because the sale's going on too long.'

The Mouton 1946 comes up. No mention is made of the repair to the label and it goes for £1,500 to a Swiss buyer in the middle of the room, bidding for a German wine company. The next lot is a double magnum of 1947 Mouton Rothschild which fetches £1,800, twice the estimate. These are extraordinary prices and it is clear that the sale is going far better than expected.

But the prices are genuine; there is no evidence of the sort of funny play that Pat Grubb of Sotheby's has told me about. 'There are occasions when they see a rival and will go on pushing him, and then there are times when you can't prove it but you will see people pushing prices up because it will give them a game (perhaps because the château wants some publicity). It happens quite often with champagne,' says Alan.

A very fat American from Miami comes in, buys a couple of lots and waddles out again. Another American, thin, balding, bearded and apparently shattered by jetlag, stands wearily at the back of the room but wakes up sufficiently to buy three bottles of 1955 Pétrus for his store in Texas.

'Lot 213, the '49 Cheval Blanc. O my Gawd, I've got to do a little explanation here. Let's take each lot as it goes. Two bottles have slip labels, three levels upper shoulder and one mid-shoulder.

'Lot 214, ten slip labels. I'd like to know why you didn't print all this information in the catalogue [looking at Michael Broadbent]. Ha! Ha! It's getting complicated. . . .'

As Alan continues with his explanations, a couple drift into the room for whom all this talk of ullages and slip labels is complete gibberish. They have come to look at an exquisite Rubens drawing that is hanging on the wall near the rostrum, ready for next week's sale.

There is a parcel of Château Nenin 1955 (mediocre stuff, I tasted it). The first lots go for £130 per dozen, the last for £180 as buyers scramble for stock. 'It's almost always cheaper to buy the first lots,' claims Alan.

A sleek, expensive, slim, middle-aged blonde causes a minor sensation as she slips in at the back of the room, sits down beside the fat man from Miami and wraps her arms round his neck. Love is blind, for it would be hard to imagine an uglier man.

The room fills as the rarer lots come up, and empties slightly after they are sold. There is a perceptible rise and fall in the level of excitement. But you have only to walk next door to the furniture sale to get a whiff of the real big time. A rubicund caricature of an Englishman is in the rostrum, jumping the bidding up in steps of a thousand pounds at a time while various minions relay bids from telephones on the wall. A cabinet is sold for £55,000 and no one seems particularly startled.

Back in the wine auction, time is getting on. 'I think I must explain, ladies and gentlemen, I'm slowing up. Here we are at five to one and I'm only on lot 281. Bring your lunch.'

But the morning session ends shortly after 1.15, Alan having scampered through the last eighty lots in just over twenty minutes. 'The Americans bid slower than the English,' he says later. He clearly would not enjoy the protracted day-long affair of the annual Hospices de Beaune auction.

Broadbent takes the afternoon session of old rarities and vinous accessories. He is fast, authoritative and enlivens the sale with occasional flashes of wit, but I haven't the patience to sit through it all. I leave a commission to bid for a bar corkscrew, irresistibly described as 'Loftus The Rapid', and run for the train back home.

The sale comprised 583 lots, ranging from the very grandest wines to a patent bottle lock. The vintages spanned one and a half centuries, including port made in the year of Waterloo and claret of most of the great harvests from 1870 to 1971. It was an impressive range, demonstrating the auctioneer's dominance of the market in mature claret (and other wines) which so greatly infuriates some of the traditional merchants.

But this market was one that had been largely abandoned by the merchants, deterred by high interest rates from investing in long-term stock, and in its present form it is entirely the creation of the two great auction houses. What merchant, after all, could have accumulated so wide a range as was brought together in this sale, largely from private cellars?

The market in such wines is certainly a curious one. The level of prices is set by rarity and prestige and the competitive acquisitiveness of rich collectors, rather than by any attempt at an objective assessment of quality, but that is not the point. For without such a market and the excitement that it generates, the public interest in fine wine would certainly be less and this might well affect prices of the more accessible classics (the 1970 clarets, for example) or even the young vintages which form the stock-in-trade of the merchants. And it may well be argued that the success of the auctioneers in establishing a stable market for mature vintages may even encourage the merchants to resume their traditional role of holding wine for the long term, reasonably sure that they will eventually be able to sell at a decent profit.

Meanwhile, many of those who mutter crossly about auctioneers are happy to decorate their wine lists with a range of classic vintages which they have gleaned from the sale room, or to use the auction house as a dustbin for unwanted bin-ends of tired stock.

For the public the auction offers entertainment and the occasional opportunity for a bargain. But if you haven't tasted a sample of what's on offer, *caveat emptor*!

XIII
Purple Prose:
The Wine Writers

Read All About It

'If all the world were paper and all the seas were ink
If all the trees
Were bread and cheese
What would we have to drink?'

The inky schoolboy's plaintive cry should be the watchword of every scribbler. Wine writing, in particular, seems as much a plague as a profession; highly infectious and a sore trial to the world. The allure of the subject is no guarantee of readable prose. On the contrary, like much writing about other sensual pleasures, the results are often tedious technical manuals, pornography or pulp fiction. Fortunately there are exceptions.

The first serious book on wine in the English language was published just over 150 years ago, in 1833. Cyrus Redding's *History and Description of Modern Wines* is a marvellous work combining, like Hugh Johnson in our own day, an encyclopaedic grasp of facts with enthusiasm and a lively style. Ranging all over the wine-making world, he describes wine simply but with great accuracy. We can still recognize 'a taste of the raspberry' in Volnay or 'the sweet odour of violets' in Côte Rôtie. My favourite phrase concerns the wines of Margaux which, claims Redding, 'when in perfection, in a favourable year, have great fineness, a rich colour and a soft bouquet which is balmy on the palate'.

Such vivid and succinct description is a rarity in the literature of wine. Far commoner are flowery imprecisions, or dull repetitions of the same hackneyed formulae. Worst of all, perhaps, is agency prose, the cloying breathlessness of the copywriter. As the wine merchants woo the wine journalists these regrettably deathless phrases slip easily from advertisement to editorial. For most wine writing, however grand its pretensions, is really an extension of journalism. Since the promise of free lunches, occasional trips abroad and plenty of alcohol is sufficient to lure hardened habitués out of El Vino's, there is more than a sufficiency of would-be wine writers in Fleet Street. A great many wine articles and not a few books are compiled in a hurry by idle hacks who are content to meet their deadlines by subscribing their names to the glowing terms of the press release. The real authors of their columns are the PR departments of the large wine companies.

A much more serious category consists of moonlighters from the wine trade; professionals in the business who write books and articles on the side. Some are uninspired drudges, but this group also includes such diversely entertaining characters as Gerald Asher, Michael Broadbent and Steven Spurrier; writers whose combined experience of wine would be impossible to match outside the trade.

Finally, there is that relatively recent phenomenon, the true specialist wine writer. Hugh Johnson is the best known and most successful example, having followed his bestselling *Wine* with the even better selling *World Atlas of Wine* (over one and a half million copies sold, in ten languages) and then the series of *Pocket Wine Books* and the encyclopaedic *Wine Companion*. He is brilliant at popularizing his subject without trivialization: everyone in the wine trade refers constantly to his books to check some vital detail, only to emerge several pages later, seduced by the fluency of his prose.

Hugh does have international rivals (the Dutchman Hubrecht Duijker, the Italian Veronelli, the American Burton Anderson) but wine writing remains a peculiarly English speciality. Its appeal has a lot in common with that of gardening (Hugh Johnson's other love), and it is not surprising to see English women emerging as the new authorities on the subject, vinous heirs to Gertrude Jekyll and Vita Sackville-West.

Their arrival has added a further layer of confusion to the wine trade's already muddled state of mind about the writers. On the one hand, journalists tend to be regarded as parasites who do nothing but complain about the quality of lunch, get boorishly drunk and steal the samples. On the other, they are clearly a necessary evil and must be wooed for their good opinion. For years, the Institute of Masters of Wine forbade anyone outside the trade (i.e. journalists) to sit the examination. They finally relented in 1984 with predictably pleasing results. Top honours in that year's exam went to Maureen Ashley, a brilliant taster attached to the Wine Standards Board (not exactly an outsider but not mainstream wine trade either) and she was joined in the new group of Masters of Wine by Jancis Robinson, who sat the exam when seven months pregnant, having completed her revision during breaks from filming the second series of *The Wine Programme* for Channel 4. Jancis promptly announced that, having won the right to the coveted letters, she was *not* going to use them.

Her success proved what was already obvious, that the top wine writers are often more widely informed than most professionals in the trade. They have the time and the opportunity to go to more tastings, visit more vineyards, catch the news when it's hot. They get invited everywhere because the producers recognize their influence and understand that a leisurely lunch with a few journalists pays better dividends than innumerable tastings for the trade. So the writers often get wind of the latest technical innovations or taste the products of up-and-coming wine regions well ahead of the merchants. As a result, they no longer simply reflect the awareness of the trade; they actually help to form public taste and to educate the professionals.

This influence can be malign (writers on both sides of the Atlantic have unfairly damned particular vintages), but mostly it acts as a catalyst to accelerate the appreciation of better wine. Rioja and California are two important regions that owe a great deal of their recent success to the enthusiasm of a few influential scribblers.

Recognizing this, the most innovative wine merchants are continually in touch with the top journalists, passing on news of their latest discoveries and picking up information in return. That at least is the theory. In practice, shared enthusiasm leads to friendship and friendship leads to gossip. I once spent the best part of dinner with the wine correspondent of *The Times*, arguing about different types of potato!

Edmund Penning-Rowsell

When I first met Edmund Penning-Rowsell I found him rather formidable: bristly (fierce eyebrows, moustache, tufts of hair on the cheeks); brusque; authoritative. He could easily have been the subject of one of those 'Spy' cartoons in *Vanity Fair*; an irascible clubman, entitled 'Claret'. It was only after a good many years that I summoned up the courage to call him Eddie, and that I came to appreciate the wonderfully entertaining layers of his personality which combines, in a characteristically English way, the habits of a professional, the aptitudes of a gifted amateur and the nineteenth-century idealism of the Arts and Crafts Movement.

The surface is certainly deceptive. This apparently conservative product of a famous school (Marlborough), member of a great London club (The Travellers), habitué of Glyndebourne, Chairman of the Wine Society and author of the classic book on Bordeaux is a lifelong socialist who got sacked from his wartime job in an aircraft factory for being an active trade unionist. Of course it seemed perfectly natural to 'EPR' (since union meetings were held in Bristol) that he should drop in beforehand on his wine merchant to taste a few vintages of old claret. 'In my day everyone who was interested in fine wine had an account at Avery's.' It is equally typical, both of the paper and the man, that Penning-Rowsell should be wine correspondent of that bastion of capitalism, the *Financial Times*. Nothing about him is quite what it seems.

When *The Wines of Bordeaux* first appeared in 1969 it became an immediate classic (despite appalling distribution by the publishers); so much so that by the following year it was already being referred to as if it had the authority of antiquity. As a young trainee in the wine trade I was told to read it from cover to cover, and was surprised to learn in the introduction that 'Like most other books on wine this one has been written by an interested amateur'. He also happened to be Chairman of the International Exhibition Co-operative Wine Society, that remarkable organization which he has described as 'the oldest and largest wine club in the world'.

His interest in wine and membership of the Wine Society date back nearly fifty years to the time of his marriage, but Penning-Rowsell was not brought up as a connoisseur of great vintages. Quite the reverse. His parents were divorced when he was eleven and when he was just seventeen there was suddenly no money to continue his education (it was the aftermath of the Great Crash), let alone buy the other luxuries of life. EPR left Marlborough and got a job on the high Tory *Morning Post* at £2 per week.

As with so many illustrious (and notorious) contemporaries, the hardships of these times confirmed his political inclinations. He declared his sympathies at school. 'I wouldn't join the OTC at Marlborough but I wasn't a pacifist.' At that time, at that school, it was a decision of real courage. The succeeding half century has modified the expression but not the character of his beliefs. 'Meg's brother [Meg is his wife] fought in the International Brigade in Spain. We were brought up in the thirties. We haven't changed our views.'

They met in 1933 and were married four years later. Meg was working at the BBC but in those days a woman employee's marriage led to dismissal from Reith's empire. Her immediate boss softened the blow with the gift of some non-vintage Moulin à Vent and proper wineglasses from Berry Bros. Shortly afterwards a friend introduced Penning-Rowsell to the Wine Society and he began to correspond with Ronald Avery and Charles Walter Berry, the leading wine merchants of the day. It was Berry who presented EPR with his first cellar book.

Its pages record a pretty mixed bunch of wines in those early years, including the casks of Muscadet, Tavel and St Emilion that they imported from a shipper in Nantes, and bottled with the help of their friends in the cellar of their Bloomsbury publisher's premises. 'We had a jolly time and it didn't turn to vinegar.' Gradually they started buying and tasting more serious stuff. 'The '24 Grand-Puy-Lacoste was the first wine that really excited me. It tasted like blackcurrants. Now of course I think that blackcurrants taste like claret!'

The early years of the war were spent working at aircraft factories and organizing a trade union amongst the clerical staff to combat the 'frightful conditions' that he found there. He furthered his friendship with Ronald Avery and 'his hardly treated Number Two, Bill Newton', and he steadily accumulated a serious cellar. In 1943 he joined the army ('He was the only person who looked really distinguished in battledress as a private,' says Meg) and he spent D-Day as a signalman in a wireless hut overlooking Langstone harbour. 'Luckily they had an efficient American radio ham in each station.'

As the war drew to a close, EPR was promoted to Staff Sergeant and moved into army education, ensconced in Welback Abbey, lecturing on economics and recent British history. 'He's widely read,' says Meg. 'Put that in.'

And then it was back to publishing. 'There were many similarities between the wine trade and the book trade. People who were great rivals were very friendly to each other.' But there were other, less pleasing parallels, for in publishing as in the wine trade, the 1950s and 60s were a time of endless takeovers. In 1950 Penning-Rowsell lost his job as a director of Frederick Muller when the company was devoured by a 'dreadful man', Packer senior, the boss of Australian Consolidated Press. He moved via Batsfords to Hultons, whose mainstay was the *Eagle*, the enormously successful children's comic produced by that strange cleric, the Reverend Marcus Morris. After starting the Studio Vista series for Hultons, Penning-Rowsell eventually found himself working for another cleric, Tim (later Lord) Beaumont, who put in a school friend of his to run the company. 'In those days you were assumed to be able to be a wine merchant if you could drink the stuff, and a publisher if you could read.' It was at this point (1963) that Penning-Rowsell finally quit. His swansong in publishing was to organize the World Book Fair at Earls Court in 1964. It was opened by the Queen. 'I shook her hand. She seemed terribly nervous,' claims Eddie.

He was fifty and unemployed but he had already begun to write occasional wine articles for *Country Life* and anonymous reviews for the *TLS*, and he compiled a brief history of the Wine Society of which he had just been elected Chairman. Penning-Rowsell used to drive up to London from Oxfordshire with George Rainbird. 'He was a packager of books, very keen on wine and a great friend of André Simon. He became president of the Wine & Food Society' (an office now held by Michael Broadbent). During one of those drives Rainbird mentioned that he was looking for authors to write a couple of books, on claret and on burgundy. 'So Harry Yoxall wrote the book on burgundy. I did Bordeaux.'

Penning-Rowsell was clear from the start that his was going to be 'a different sort of wine book'. 'Different' meant 'scholarly'. Eddie spent months researching in the British Museum and he and his family took their brief holidays in Bordeaux, camping in the garden at Château Langoa Barton. The result was an extraordinary monograph, combining a fascinating historical survey with sections on geology and viticulture, on the wine firms of Bordeaux, on the great châteaux; chapters on each of the major regions; notes on the vintages, way back to the eighteenth century; appendices of statistical information. It was a classic, but it was also twice as long as George Rainbird had expected.

So began a wretched saga of muddles and mismanagement that must have seemed a nightmare to an author who had spent half his life in the publishing business. The book was often out of print in England and took ages to appear at all in America. So furtive was its publication that it is a wonder anyone ever read *The Wines of Bordeaux*, at least until the recent, revised and enlarged editions. But slowly the sales figures mounted and the reputation spread. In fact, the latest edition appeared in 1985. This most English of all the wine writers took his first trip to the vineyards of California in 1981 and found himself something of a star in the States. 'Americans like my book because they love facts. I love facts too!'

These details emerged as Eddie decanted the wine for dinner. I had suggested lunch but he insisted that I come and stay the night. 'The wine's always better in the evening.' So there I was being offered a choice of marvels and ending up with a 1976 Montrachet from Baron Thénard and the 1948 La Mission-Haut-Brion. Meg called quietly for him to hurry before the supper spoiled.

She looks, at first glance, like the wife of an old-fashioned vicar, gently unadventurous and very kind. As with Eddie, appearances deceive, for she is quiet but very entertaining, intelligent and independent minded. Amongst many unsuspected qualities she is a good and adventurous cook. The *salade tiède* was followed by a wonderful dish of pigeon breasts ('I asked Raymond Blanc of the Quatr' Saisons for the recipe').

The Montrachet was glorious: a suggestion of marzipan on the nose; long, complex and elegant on the palate. Quite beautiful.

'You ask my political views,' grinned Eddie. 'I don't believe that the Tory devils should have all the best wines!'

The 1948 La Mission was served in a pretty, eighteenth-century decanter. 'I last drank this wine nine years ago. . . . I loved the '48s but then they went acid. I remember the '49 very well. We were in Paris and had lunch with the Woltners [owners of La Mission]. It was my birthday and they gave us the '49. A marvellous wine.'

This bottle, at any rate, hadn't gone acid. Extraordinarily dark and youthful in colour, it had that dense bouquet typical of La Mission. 'Blackcurrants,' muttered EPR. Another sniff: 'I always think of hot brick-dust with Graves.' Meg said, 'Tarry', and I agreed, thinking of Barolo. We argued peacefully. On the palate it had a vigorous animal character, an intensity and a wonderful sweet warmth that developed into a lingering richness as the wine opened up in the glass.

Stimulated by this classic claret, Penning-Rowsell's anecdotes continued to flow. 'Christian Cruse was a marvellous man. We had lunch with him and his wife in his house. I always remember what we tasted. The first wine was the Léoville-Poyferré, Vin de Goutte [rosé], the 1898. He apologised because the 1878 had been finished! At the end of lunch, after a series of nineteenth-century bottles, he lifted from the mantelpiece another decanter, "*La perle de ma cave*", the 1875 Lafite. It was the most marvellous wine!'

Inevitably, the talk turned to Ronald Avery, that much-loved but often wholly infuriating merchant. 'Ronald said (and I didn't learn this until after his death) that he liked going abroad with me more than anyone else. I said "It didn't feel like that the the time!". . . . At home he used to go to bed very late and get into the office by lunch-time. . . . Ronald really liked claret best, but the problems of burgundy fascinated him. But Bordeaux, claret, was what we would usually drink together. . . . André Simon was probably the only man Ronald was not critical about but he taught me more about wine than anyone else.' Eddie barked with laughter and looked, momentarily, like a drawing by Georg Grosz.

After a brief detour to Wagnerian opera, to which both Eddie and Meg are addicted, the conversation reverted to wine and the power of the wine writer. Penning-Rowsell was doubtful. 'I would have thought in this country it's not very great. The Americans are much more interested to learn than the British. They are very keen. But I've never had an example of a wine that I recommend being sold out. I suppose, cumulatively, wine writing in England has done a lot for wine.' The French, at any rate, appreciate what he has done. In 1981 they made him a *Chevalier de l'Ordre National du Mérite*, an honour he shares with Michael Broadbent.

His fortnightly piece in the *Financial Times* tends to concern itself with general areas of vinous interest, rather than providing a shopping list for his readers, but he does regularly recommend the better sources of supply, with one notable exception: Penning-Rowsell has never mentioned the Wine Society in print. It is a matter of professional honour, the refusal to use his position to advertise the organization of which he has been chairman for over twenty years.

'I was attracted to the sort of society that it was,' he says: a cooperative, owned by its members. When he first joined the Society, five of the eight members of the Committee of Management were over seventy-five and they exercised very remote control. All that has changed and he, in particular, has been an active chairman, initiating a great many improvements: better wines, greater efficiency, more attractive and informative lists. 'Christopher Bradshaw of Eyre & Spottiswoode [and of Christie's Wine Publications] helps to design them. I don't *do* these things but I stimulated them. And I've cultivated very much relations with our members.' He personally signs a letter of welcome to every one of the thousands of new members. But his most important recommendation [in 1964] was to move the Wine Society out of its scattered cellars all over London, and to group its operations under one roof, at Stevenage. This was bitterly opposed 'by the conservatives on the Committee, who demanded an inquiry', but Penning-Rowsell prevailed. 'We made a great loss that year. It was a terrible time, but we pulled through' and no one now doubts the wisdom of the move. Later on, when the Society needed further cash for expansion, Eddie suggested that they ask the members for contributions to an interest-free loan. To the surprise of many, the scheme met with a tremendous response and has been repeated since.

As we finished dinner Penning-Rowsell glanced towards the empty decanter. 'I think I've been very lucky that I drank at a time when it was possible to buy fine wines (including old wines) at not very high cost. Now it's impossible. My professor son is reasonably well off yet to buy first growths *en primeur* is beyond what he feels he would want to pay. I used to buy one dozen first growth claret a year, at a pound a bottle duty-paid. I was earning £700 a year. There were opportunities open then. Cheval Blanc '47 I bought for 22/6 [£1.12½]!'

The house is full of mementoes of this enviable drinking life: empty bottles annotated with tasting notes on the wine and the company in which it was enjoyed. In my bedroom (William Morris wallpaper, rather cold) the dead men included a 1906 Haut-Brion, 1888 Margaux, 1870 Schloss Johannisberg and a nineteenth-century sherry from the cellars of Sir George Meyrick.

In the morning there were two pots of marmalade on the breakfast table, the lighter one made by Meg; the darker, more caramelized version by Eddie. The talk was of opera. 'Late Verdi is marvellous. And Wagner, so *interesting. Tristan* is the most marvellous opera; the frustration of love and passion. . . . With Mozart or Verdi you don't need to know the words but with Wagner you have to understand what's going on. They just stand there and sing. And at the end of the act they kill each other or something. We've been to Bayreuth three times (and those Baroque churches that I love too) and I go to Glyndebourne every year. I would love to go to the Edinburgh Festival but I always feel that the food must be so bad!'

Walking in the garden with Meg I admired a vast yew hedge. 'Eddie and Edmund, our son, clip it once a year in August or September, talking about wine the entire time!'

Shortly before I left, Eddie put on a recording of *Der Rosenkavalier* and played the famous trio near the end, when the Marschallin resigns herself to her fate. He stood there sightless, lost in the music, and as it ended he raised his hand and then let it fall heavily to his side, echoing her words, *'In Gottes Namen. . .'*; God has decided.

'Well, there you are,' he said. 'It's time for the train.'

XIV
Enthusiasm

(To be read with glass in hand)

*'He had known the classification of the Médoc Crus by heart
and would recite them like so many lines of poetry:
Château Latour, Château Rauzan Segla, Château Rauzan-
Gassies, Château Léoville Lascases;
Château Ducru Beaucaillou, Château Montrose. . . .'*

Sybille Bedford: *A Favourite of the Gods*

Gardeners and wine lovers have a lot in common. Sensual and
aesthetic pleasure is at the heart of the matter, the delight in colour
and scent and taste, but there is also an intellectual challenge: the
fascination of species and sub-species, of identifying, classifying,
comparing varieties; of knowing the meaning of thousands of mys-
terious names. And then there are the pottering pleasures: brows-
ing through catalogues; rummaging through junk shops for glasses
or flowerpots; rambling conversation with like-minded enthusiasts.
You learn generosity (plantsmen and wine lovers regard their treasures as things to be shared, not hoarded) and you learn patience:
planting trees, like laying down claret, is an act of faith.

The starting point is essentially the same – the grower – and there
tend to be similarities of character between the people involved.
Gentle old Wakem Rickeard and his son Michael growing all manner of country favourites in their tiny nursery at Yoxford, or Peter
Beales with his world famous collection of old-fashioned roses at
Attleborough, are quintessentially English characters, but it
requires no great effort of the imagination to transpose them into
the vineyards of Europe.

Then there are the amateurs. There was a wonderful picture on the back page of *The Times* a few years ago of Humphrey Brooke, immaculately dressed in an indefinably eccentric and old-fashioned way, sitting beneath an *enormous* and very prickly bush – a vast rose, throwback to prehistoric times that had mysteriously emerged amongst his wonderful collection of old-fashioned varieties, in the untamed jungle of his garden at Clayden.

Pre-phylloxera claret will not, alas, reproduce itself though it does occasionally turn up from long-forgotten cellars, faded but still full of character like the last, indomitable survivor of an old and famous family: but the world of wine continues to produce characters like Humphrey Brooke, 'enthusiasts to the point of mania', as the writer Sybille Bedford puts it.

She is one such and her books are full of vivid vinous moments, like drinking Krug champagne with onion soup, or (cruel fate) having to endure cheap Sauternes in Mexico while sitting above a cellar of 1900 Lafite and Margaux. One of the most entertaining episodes is the story of Mena's wine in *A Favourite of the Gods*; a wonderful set-piece centred on a famous Italian rarity: 'Barone Barbasoli's Private Bottling straight from the Gaiole vineyards, Gran Riserva, Stravecchio, Classico and all the rest of it. . . .' It is wholly fictitious, a Shandian joke that sent me scurrying on a wild goose chase through the reference books.

This remarkable writer appears modestly on our mailing list as Bedford, Mrs S., with an address in Chelsea. She has bought from us occasionally and keeps some of her wine in our cellars but I had no idea who she was, even when I chanced to sit next to her at a wine dinner at L'Escargot. I greatly enjoyed her company and was spellbound by the stories she told when I asked how she had come to appreciate wine. The next day a friend, a tremendous fan, thrust her copy of *A Legacy* into my hands. A week or two later I encountered Mrs Bedford at Christie's, at a tasting organized by Steven Spurrier, and shortly afterwards I eased a tedious period of illness by reading all her novels and her wonderful account of a Mexican journey, *A Visit to Don Ottavio*.

The acquaintance, becoming friendship, is both characteristic of the way such things go and atypical, because the mathematics of the business are against us. For every grower who is a friend there must be hundreds or thousands of customers who buy their wine from me but remain anonymous. It is a great pity, for when they do reveal themselves they present such an extraordinary range of character and interest. Few have led so colourful a life as Sybille Bedford, or are as eccentric as B'Indy Huang from Taiwan who for years sent us curious limericks every time we produced a new wine list or vintage report. Some customers are undeniably dull. But the appreciation of wine is one of the earthier virtues of civilization; enthusiasts tend to be good company.

If *we* have limits placed on our ability to communicate individually with them, *they* have no inhibitions about reminding us that there are far more wine experts outside the trade than in it. Our customers write to us a lot, praising, criticizing, making suggestions, and I have frequently benefited from their advice. Even the dreaded 'I brought this bottle back from my holiday' (bane of a wine merchant's life) can lead to exciting discoveries. And we can never afford to ignore our customers' hobby-horses lest they turn professional and set up as rivals!

The borderline in any case is blurred. Like plant collectors roaming the foothills of the Himalayas or the hidden valleys of South America in search of unusual specimens (which they bring back, propagate and distribute to fellow gardeners), the passionate amateur of wine goes exploring the vineyards. A case or two brought back from the first visit becomes a van-load to be shared with friends. Eventually such enthusiasts discover that they are running a wine business, like the dentist and doctor team of Robin and Judith Yapp or like Justin de Blank, who expanded a superior grocery into an empire that encompasses food shops, a bakery and a couple of restaurants in London plus another restaurant, their home, in Norfolk.

He and his wife Melanie go tramping round the wine regions of France twice a year, sometimes by themselves, often with friends. Last time they took along an 84-year-old widow, 'one of those tough, indomitable, East Coast Americans'. Justin brought wine for the restaurants, a limited range from reputable growers. 'The French still trade in a nineteenth-century way. If they like you, the chances that they will rip you off are reduced.'

We were sitting amidst the remains of a protracted breakfast on a wet Sunday at Shipdam, tasting a couple of samples that I had brought for him.

'We used to buy Madame Faller's Alsace wines. She's not at all a *cracheuse*; she swallows. After going out to lunch *she* drives back absolutely sober and *you* turn round the corner and go to sleep for twenty-four hours. She's absolutely lovely and very fond of Melanie.'

The object of this devotion raised her head from the newspaper as a stream of water cascaded down outside the window. 'Justin likes her bosom!' laughed Melanie. 'Look, the gutter's overflowing.'

Is this the wine trade? Of course not, it's *my* wine trade.

The view is partial, incomplete and unrepresentative for this is a gallery of characters whose lives have happened to intersect my own. There is, after all, no point in wasting print on the bland mediocrity of mass market blends or the complexities of import documentation; in such matters the wine trade is indistinguishable from many others. The distinctive and invigorating thing is that it is full of enthusiasts who share a passion for the commodity in which they deal, for wine itself.

This mania develops at any age, in many circumstances; there is no predictable path. Hence my final story, one that is quite outside the common experience of wine but which conveys, better than any other that I know, its magic.

Sybille Bedford was brought up to love wine; in Europe, between the wars, she was a precociously adult child. Her mother (beautiful but flighty) was a bolter: she left her much older husband, Sybille's father, when the child was two. They were living then in Baden, 'in a small seventeenth-century château, stuffed with antiques'. He was a collector who had spent all his adult life in France and Italy and settled on Baden as being the closest approximation to not really living in Germany, his homeland. When Sybille was six her father announced that he was ruined. The servants were dismissed, the horses were sold and donkeys were harnessed uncomfortably in their shafts. The brilliant social life came to an abrupt end; 'everything was gone'. Father and daughter camped on the first floor of the house in the erstwhile morning room, served by a woman from the village who did everything from milking the goat to preparing awful meals on a wood- and coal-burning stove. Her cooking was a terrible penance for a man who had spent hours in discussion with the great chefs of Europe and who advocated, well in advance of his time, the spirit of classic simplicity that pervades the best modern cuisine.

The bright moment of the day, and the time of terror, came in the evening. Sybille at the age of six or seven was her father's companion and butler. They dined together, like adults. He had ceased to send out for beer (too expensive) so they steadily worked their way through a cellar of classic claret. Each night the child was sent downstairs (two storeys) to fetch the bottle for the morrow's dinner. The house was dark, there was no electricity, and the flickering candle illuminated the debris of a collector's life. 'There were crucifixes everywhere' and there was talk of ghosts. Sybille was terrified. The one thing she must not do was break the bottle but equally she dare not let go the candle. So the ghosts presented a fearful problem because she knew (the village woman had told her) that she would only be safe if she made the sign of the cross and prayed for the repose of their souls. She had no spare hand, so she decided that her father's wrath was more dreadful than the dark. The bottle was held in her left hand and the candle in her right, ready to be dropped if she had to cross herself. Steadfastly she made her way upstairs.

Once she was there the terror ceased and the joy began. Her father decanted the rested bottle from the previous evening's expedition and then, surrounded by dogs to whom he tossed the choicest morsels of the *gigot* (their own 'Parma lamb', smoked on their own fire), they tasted, discussed and drank their claret in all seriousness, as enthusiasts. The nanny, brief survivor of more prosperous times, suggested that the child should mix her wine with water. She was promptly sacked (it was the last straw, he knew she was a secret ally of his departed wife). Alone in the candlelight, father and daughter enjoyed the happiest hour of their day.

He died when she was ten and Sybille was reunited with her mother in Italy. At certain points their life seemed to involve a great deal of travelling and she often found herself taking long train journeys, quite alone, from one corner of Europe to another. These were the only times that she was given any money, and Sybille used to spend it in the grand restaurants of the railway termini, in the intervals between connections. The head waiters were amused but they got on well with the self-possessed thirteen-year-old who allowed them to advise her on the menu but chose the wine by herself: 'half a bottle of good claret; nothing that she would have felt to be outrageous, nothing like Haut-Brion or Lafite, but something in the order of a third or fourth growth of the Médoc. . . . She loved the shapes of bottles and of course the romantic names and the pictures of the pretty manor houses on the labels, and she loved the link with rivers and hillsides and climates and hot years, and the range of learning and experiment afforded by wine's infinite variety; but what she loved more than these was the taste – of peach and earth and honeysuckle and raspberries and spice and cedarwood and pebbles and truffles and tobacco leaf; and the happiness, the quiet ecstasy that spreads through heart and limbs and mind.*

* Sybille Bedford: *A Compass Error.*

Index